Happy Reading!
Love,
Cynthia DeLuca

Meatballs and Minestrone

Cynthia Jean DeLuca

© 2017 Cynthia Jean DeLuca
All rights reserved.

ISBN: 1537174665
ISBN 13: 9781537174662
Library of Congress Control Number: **2017916910**
LCCN Imprint Name: **CreateSpace Independent Publishing Platform, North Charleston, SC**

For my brother, Lee, and my sisters, Donna and Emma, who have and always will be my precious gifts. And for Mom and Dad in heaven, who always encouraged me to follow my dreams.

Prologue

Once upon a time, there was a little girl who dreamed big dreams. The little girl was bullied throughout her childhood because she lived on a farm, was chubby, and did not have many clothes. But the little girl kept dreaming. She dreamed of being a teacher, singing beautiful songs, helping others, and writing stories that would make people smile.

Then one day the dreams took a rest as the young woman married and raised a family. She helped her parents in their time of need and kept herself busy. Even though the dreams were resting, a subtle stirring began tugging at her heart. The stirring got stronger and stronger until the young woman could not ignore it any longer. As her children grew up, she thought and thought, talked to her husband, and prayed for guidance.

Now a middle-aged woman, she knew what she had to do. She enrolled in college for the first time in her life. It wasn't easy, but she worked hard and soon walked across the stage to receive her degree in special education.

She entered her first classroom at the age of forty-two and never looked back. After twenty-three years in the classroom, she retired with the overwhelming feeling that she had made a difference.

As she took her last walk down the school

hallway, past the office, and out the door, a stirring started tickling her heart once again. She smiled as she drove away from her beloved school and thought about her dream of making a difference with her words. She knew what she had to do as she took out her yellow tablet and started to write. The woman had written a few children's stories with more to come when a warm feeling filled her heart. She bowed her head and said a simple prayer and then picked up her pencil and started writing inspirational short stories: stories from her heart, stories that would make those reading smile or maybe laugh out loud.

And yet the stirring continued as the senior

woman yearned to speak to anyone who would listen. The Wednesday Chats came to the woman as she slept, and she knew in her heart that just maybe she might make a difference in someone's life speaking on topics that were near and dear to her heart. And still the dreams kept stirring!

This little story is not about bragging. It is a story about dreams. It is a story about a little girl who never stopped dreaming and never will.

I am the little girl who was bullied, the young woman who raised her family, the middle-aged woman who went to college, and the senior who writes and speaks, hoping to make a difference.

Life is a journey; dreams are part of that journey. Live them, enjoy each day, and then dream some more.

Love,

Cynthia

Part One

Memories from the Farm

My Special Angel

The White Stove

Little Sister

Don't Name the Puppies

The Rogue Mower

Can of Worms

Laughter for One

The Rabble-Rouser Rooster

Laughter for Two

Winter on the Farm

Christmas on Ayers Road

Part Two

Memories of Mom

Happy Birthday to Our Angel

A Piece of My Heart

The Bear Who Brought Me Peace

The Incredible Ethel

A Phone Call, a Visit, and a Blue Butterfly

The Christmas Orange

Part Three

Stories from My Heart

What My Teapot Taught Me

Those Who Serve, Those Who Wait

Minestrone for the Heart

The Look of Not Knowing

Mountains to Climb

On the Wings of the Cardinal

L'amour est la réponse (Love Is the Answer)

Meatballs Filled with Love

Friday: A Day of Lessons

The Magic of a Bowl of Soup

Part One

Memories from the Farm

My Special Angel

I was born in 1948 to a beautiful young woman named Roberta Lorraine Transue. My biological father wanted to marry Mom, but it was not meant to be. During that era, having a baby out of wedlock was far from acceptable. Although Mom knew the road would be hard, she was not afraid.

Mom worked hard—very hard—but it was not enough to pay rent, buy food, pay utilities, and take care of my needs, so we lived with relatives. Mom was one of fifteen children, so it wasn't hard to find an aunt or uncle to live with.

I must be honest and say I don't have a

good recollection of some of the aunts and uncles we lived with until we moved to a little village near Nazareth. I was four.

We moved in on a Saturday, unpacked, and settled in. I loved sharing a room with Mom. She had long, wavy auburn hair and the most beautiful sparkling blue eyes. Soon Monday arrived, and Mom had to go to work. My uncle also left on a job that took him away from home for periods of time. Mom hugged and kissed me and then walked to the door, turned, and blew a kiss. Little did she know my life was about to change. And so, it began…

After Mom left for work, my aunt fed me breakfast and asked me to go out to the small two-sided porch and wait for her children to come out. They never did. I remember looking in the window at them having fun and playing games. Although I knocked several times, they ignored me. My lunch was brought out to me. I could use the bathroom but had to return to the little porch. My aunt allowed me to come into the house right when Mom came home from work.

Tears…

As soon as Mom walked through the door, I ran to her with tears streaming down my face. She honestly thought I was excited to see her. Before dinner, I told her everything about my day. Mom questioned my aunt, but the answer was that I had an overactive imagination. Mom hugged me and told me that Tuesday would be better—that I just had to get used to being in a different home.

The next four days were repeats: eat breakfast, go to the porch, in before Mom got home. Each afternoon when Mom returned home, there were tears and begging. Begging to move.

Mom to the Rescue…

Each night when I cried, I saw Mom looking at my aunt, saying, "This is not like Cindy to cry like this. Something is wrong here!"

Friday, the day started as the other four had, except it was a damp, rainy day. Mom hugged me and told me that she would be home soon. The routine started: breakfast, porch sitting, and a lot of shivering. Suddenly, I saw a car pull up in front of the house. It was Mom. She came home early and found me sitting on the porch. I don't know who cried harder that day: me or Mom. I was saved!

Moving On…

Mom made a phone call, and then she and I packed. Soon my aunt Mae and uncle Charlie arrived to take Mom and me to our new home. I could not wait! They lived along the river and had a huge screened-in porch. As soon as the car stopped, I ran into the house and found the bathroom. As I was doing what I had to do, I heard water splashing. I pulled back the shower curtain, and much to my surprise, I saw several catfish swimming around the tub! I loved it!

As the Story Goes...

Eventually, Mom started dating a man from the Philadelphia area named Lee Brodt. He was smitten with Mom, and I was sure she was with him. Mom once told me that I refused to call him Mr. Brodt or even Lee. My name for this tall mans was...Man. Mom said I would say very little around him, and if I did say anything, it would be, "Hi, Man."

As the weeks went by, Mom and Man began spending more time together. I missed Mom. Man was taking her away from me; at least that was what I thought. Man was good to me. He would often try to talk to me, but I would become very shy. However, he never gave up.

Soon, I went to Philadelphia to meet his relatives. Shyness crept in again, and I clung to Mom. Man kept trying, and slowly I started to look forward to his visits, rides in the car with him and Mom, getting ice cream, and sitting by the river. However, I continued to call him Man.

The Wedding…

Soon, Mom talked to me about how much she loved Man and that they were going to be married. My cousin Martha and her husband stood up for them at Reverend Floyd Shafer's home in Tatamy. Mom wore a pink jacket and skirt, and Man wore a light-brown suit. Mom and Man were married on June 26, 1954.

The Move…

We moved to North Hills near Philadelphia. Although our apartment was small, it was cozy. I even had my own room. Mom told me it would be okay to call Man "Dad," but I was not sure until our first Halloween.

It was a dark, cold night, and Mom had taken me out to trick-or-treat. Man stayed home to give out treats to the children. After we returned with a full bag of treats, I changed and then settled in to watch television. Trick or treat was over, but I still heard voices outside.

Suddenly, something hit our front window. It sounded as if the window was going to break. I called out to Man, but this time, I said, "Daddy, someone is trying to break the window. I'm afraid!" Just then, Dad walked over to the couch and held me in his arms. Thank you, Dad, for protecting me.
My Special Angel…

That Halloween night, Dad became my angel for the first time. I felt safe in his arms. When I think back, I realize he became my angel first when he met Mom, fell in love, and married her. Because of his love for Mom and me, we became a family.

The next few years, our family grew with

the arrival of my sisters, Donna and then Emma, and finally my brother, Lee. I loved them dearly when they were each born, and I love them even more now. Dad never treated me any differently from his biological children. We had rules to follow, and above all he expected the four of us to be respectful. He never called me his stepdaughter. I was always his daughter.

As Dad aged, his health deteriorated, and all four of us helped to take care of him. We would have done anything for him. When Mom became sick, we were all there to help her too. We took care of our parents until they took their last breaths. We would do it a million times over for the two we loved so much.

My Heartfelt Thoughts…

I want to thank you, Dad, on this Father's Day, 2017, for loving Mom, which led to loving me. Thank you for giving me three gifts that I cherish each day: Donna, Emma, and Lee. Thank you for not treating me any differently from my siblings. Thank you for teaching me, encouraging me, and always being ready to listen. Thank you for celebrating with me and crying with me when Lambert died. Thank you for your laugh and thank you for buying the boxed lots of books at the auctions you loved so much. Because of those books, I developed a love of reading. You will never know how much you meant to me and still do. You may have started as "Man," but you quickly became my special angel, Dad.

One More Thought...

This story has a special place in my heart. I wrote it because this wonderful man really changed my life. When Mom was so sick, she reminded me how the story started with her and Dad. We talked about the loneliness she had felt and the bad experience I had endured for five days in a home where we truly were not wanted. She shared how much she loved Dad. Mom looked at me and said, "Dad always wanted you to be his little girl."

God blessed me with a loving dad whom I

miss so much. Until we meet again, Dad, know that I love you and always will.

The White Stove

Yesterday, I made a pot of potato soup just like my mother used to make. As I cut the potatoes and onions, my mind drifted back to my childhood and winters on the farm.

Although Mom was a very good cook, this memory is not about her delicious meals. It is about a stove that stood on the left side of two large doors that hid the old fireplace. The stove was close to a window with a green shade and a black coal bucket, which was always filled with small black nuggets ready to be shoveled into the side that warmed our kitchen.

The stove was white, with four gas burners on the right side and a combination wood-and-coal stove with cast-iron lids on the left. The lids had an indentation big enough to hold a handle that hung on a nail right in the middle of the fireplace doors. In the winter, those lids were lifted many times during the day and even during the night, depending on the outside temperature. Since we did not have a furnace, the white stove had the job of keeping the kitchen warm.

Across the room from the stove and halfway up the wall was a square-framed opening, which allowed some heat to meander up to the third step from the top of the second floor. To be honest, although the white stove worked hard with the help of our parents, it did little to bring warmth to our bedrooms. However, this little opening helped my brother, two sisters, and me to sometimes listen to the conversations of our parents and, from time to time, company. We thought we were grownups until Dad would raise his voice, making us scramble back to our beds.

Since we did not have an indoor bathroom, we bathed in the kitchen. Mom would fill a large round gray metal tub with hot water. She would always make sure the kitchen was nice and warm, and then each one of us would take our baths. When we were finished, Mom would wash our hair at the kitchen sink. The white stove worked hard on those cold nights.

In the winter, when Dad worked an afternoon shift, Mom would make us a special treat on the lid of the white stove. First, she would peel two potatoes and then slice them very thin and lightly salt them. Next, Mom would clean the lids, rub a little lard on them, and then arrange the potatoes on top. My two sisters, brother, and I would get so excited watching those potato slices sizzle on those old black lids. We would get our little colored Melmac dishes and stand in a line waiting and drooling. Those potatoes were black around the edges but oh, so delicious. My mouth is watering as I am writing this story.

I remember seeing Mom and Dad carry the

empty gray coal bucket down the creaky cellar steps, walking on long boards placed on top of the dirt floor and then returning with the bucket filled to the brim with black coal. Mom took care of the coal bucket when Dad was sick or worked the third shift. It was hard work, but Mom never complained. Although winter was the time the white stove worked the hardest, there were other seasons that come to mind.

Mom always canned her own vegetables from our garden and fruit from our very small orchard. One summer sticks out in my mind. It was the summer that Mom canned seven hundred jars! My sweet mother not only thought of us but of her many brothers and sisters who might need a little extra help. I have a funny feeling the white stove gave a sigh of relief after that experience!

I seem to have forgotten the part of the stove that also worked extremely hard: the oven. Along with baking and roasting, Mom would quite often make her own bread, which smelled heavenly when we came in from school. There is nothing better than a piece of hot bread slathered with butter.

Growing up, I did not understand or appreciate how hard Mom and Dad worked to take care of us. I know I can speak for my sisters and brother and say, "Mom, Dad, we are so grateful for your guidance and raising us to be loving and caring. Thank you for instilling in us that although we did not have a lot, we always had each other. Thank you both for showing us that when we help others, we help ourselves. Most of all, thank you for loving us and making us toe the line."

And to the white stove, when we left the farm, we left you, but you gave us a lifetime of memories, and for that we are truly grateful. When I think of how hard the white stove worked, I compare it to the many times my parents carried the bucket of coal from the cellar to keep us warm.

Little Sister

It was nearing the end of the school year, and the weather was warm and beautiful. As my school bus headed up my road and approached my house, I could hear laughter. The closer we got, the more laughter I heard.

Since I was sitting at the back of the bus, I had no clue what was going on until the bus stopped, and I peeked out the window as I headed up the aisle, horrorstruck. The loudness of the laughter filled the bus. Everyone was standing and pointing at my house. My ears started pounding, and I thought my legs were going to give out.

What was going on? As I walked down the

steps and rounded the front of the bus, my heart sank. There standing in the fenced-in play yard was my two-year-old sister, stark naked!

I walked as quickly as I could and marched into the house. Mom looked at me and smiled. I looked at her and announced that I would not be returning to school tomorrow or any other day! She looked at me with a blank stare and said, "What is wrong?"

I said, "Follow me."

As we approached the play yard, Mom could not believe her eyes. "I just put her out here! How did she get undressed so quickly?"

I looked at my sister, who was giggling. It was apparent that she did not have a care in the world. Donna was sweet and oh so tiny. Her cute brown hair and beautiful brown eyes always melted my heart. I knew that I would not be able to stay mad at her.

That night, I said a prayer that my little sister would keep her clothes on, especially if she was playing in the play yard. I also asked God to take the memory of my stark-naked sister away from all those who had seen her on that bus ride home from school. I was hoping that God would answer my prayer.

I decided I would go to school the next day and give Donna a second chance. As the bus turned onto Ayers Road, I started to feel butterflies in my stomach. The bus rumbled up the road, and soon we were at my stop. No one was laughing as the bus came to a stop. As I stepped off the last step and rounded the front of the bus, there she was, laughing and clapping her hands. There was my little sister playing in the yard with Mom, fully dressed.

My Heartfelt Thoughts…

To my little sister, Donna, the two-year-old who wouldn't keep her clothes on as a child: I loved you then, and I love you even more today!

Don't Name the Puppies!

I grew up on a small farm in rural Pennsylvania. Along with a variety of animals, we also had puppies and from time to time a few young dogs. It all started with Dad's deep love for animals of all kinds, especially the four-legged ones that barked.

It was not uncommon for Dad to bring home a stray on any given day. His love grew into a small business in which Dad would take in puppies that were not wanted or young dogs that frustrated their owners. At times, Dad had several dogs, and it was advised that he apply for a kennel license.

Dad took wonderful care of each one. He

worked with a local veterinarian who came to the farm to make sure the puppies and dogs were healthy. Most of the puppies were a mixed breed, with an occasional purebred.

Each time a new puppy or dog arrived, Dad would say, "Don't name the puppies!" I would look up at him and smile as the wheels of my brain started thinking of the perfect name for each one. Dad just didn't understand how much I loved the little darlings. Sometimes I would sneak out to the barn to catch a glimpse of the brown, black, and white daredevils rolling, wrestling, and nipping at each other. It was pure love! I wanted to keep every one of them.

The day came when the first puppy had to

leave. Dad made me stay in the house since I was already crying into my cereal. My two younger sisters were bawling their eyes out, and our baby brother was crying just because we were.

I begged Mom to let me go out to the barn to say my last good-bye to Jimmy, and although she gave me a stern look, she let me go. Dad saw me coming and smiled. He let me hug the little brown-and-white puppy who had captured my heart. I knew that Jimmy's new owners would take care of him, but I did not want him to go. I loved him so very much. I felt my tears filling my eyes, turned, and ran back to the house.

When Dad came in the house, we could tell his heart was as heavy as ours. He looked at each one of us, and with tears in his eyes, he said, "Don't name the puppies!"

During the time that Dad had his kennel, I would hear, "Don't name the puppies," many times. It was hard to take Dad's advice because of my young age. Besides, I really wanted to keep each and every one of those beautiful creatures.

My heart would break as each puppy and dog left, but I kept naming them until the day Dad could no longer keep up with the kennel. However, I continued to name every stray cat, birds that nested in the trees, and squirrels and bunnies as they scampered in the yard.

The story I wrote happened over fifty-five years ago; it is still as fresh as it was when the puppies ruled the barn. I remember that Dad made very little money on the sale of each puppy and dog. It was more important to him that the puppies and dogs were healthy and went to good, loving homes.

To my dad in heaven—guess what, Dad? I am still naming every stray cat, every bird that lands on my tree, and every squirrel and rabbit that visit my yard. You instilled a love in my heart that will never end.

The Rogue Mower

When I was around the age of twelve or thirteen, Dad bought a used riding mower. It certainly did not look like the mowers of today. I begged Dad to teach me how to drive the mower. He looked at me for a long time and then said, "No!" I looked at him for a few short minutes as I thought about what I wanted to say.

The conversation went something like this: "Dad, I really want to learn how to drive the lawn mower. Please? I will listen and do everything you tell me to do. Please, please, please? I'll be careful. I promise! Please, Dad!"

He looked at me, shook his head, and once

again answered, "*No!*"

Then I bargained: "But, Dad, I can mow the grass when you are at work. Then you can rest when you come home. Please, give me a chance. Please…"

I saw him grin. There it was—his famous grin, the grin that always led to the twinkle in his eyes. The "yes, I'm going to learn how to ride the mower" twinkle. The grin and the twinkle said it all. I just had to bide my time until Dad was ready to tell me the answer I wanted to hear.

I waited patiently for his reply when suddenly there was another voice I heard. "Lee, I don't know about this! Do you really think she is ready?" It was Mom. I hoped she would not change Dad's mind.

Dad smiled again and told me to get on the mower. He looked at Mom and said, "Let's see what she can do."

I wanted to do a little dance right there! I was so excited as I jumped on the seat and waited for Dad to start the mower. I held on to the handlebar as he started it. It chugged and made some strange noises before it settled down while I hung on for dear life. Then, suddenly, the bar became a little stuck, or maybe I turned it a little too hard. All I remember is that the mower took off in a circle!

It kept going around and around and around.

Dad kept shouting to straighten out the handlebar. Well, I turned it, and then I don't know what happened, because that rogue mower headed straight for Mom!

She started running, faster and faster, but for some strange reason, that mower kept chasing her. Picture this: Mom with her hands in the air, shaking her dish cloth, with a riding mower driven by a twelve- or thirteen-year-old, wide-eyed, scared-to-death driver who just happened to look back at her dad with the twinkly eyes and a neighbor, both laughing their heads off!

Somehow, I turned the handlebar just a little bit, and the rouge mower once again started to go around and around and around. Finally, the mower stopped. It had run out of gas. I could not wait to get off that monster. I felt a little dizzy as I got off the mower and looked to check my mother. She was catching her breath. She gave me a funny look and then started laughing, the same kind of laugh that I heard from Dad and Donna. I started laughing too as I heard Mom say,

"Cindy, you looked just like Lucy!"

(from the *I Love Lucy* show). She laughed some more as I looked at Dad. He didn't say a word. His eyes said it all. My lawn-mowing days were over!

A Can of Worms

When I was about nine years old, Dad asked if I wanted to go fishing. Of course, I said yes. I had been to the river with my aunt and uncle, but I had never gone fishing. I was really excited and predicted that I would catch the biggest fish!

Dad got an empty can, and off we went to dig up icky, really disgusting worms. I watched as Dad dug and filled the can. All I could think was "Yuck!" My face must have said it all because Dad just looked at me and started laughing.

Mom packed two sandwiches and a few snacks. She made coffee and filled Dad's red thermos with the silver cap and took out a cold bottle of orange soda for me. Soon, we were on our way to an adventure that Dad and I would never forget.

We arrived at the river and got out our little canvas seats, fishing poles, a lantern, and the bag with the sandwiches, snacks, and drinks. Oh yes, we cannot forget the icky can of worms.

After Dad got set up, he put a worm on his hook as I squinted and prayed that he would not ask me to even pick up one of those slithering brown things. I had just gotten the amen out when I heard Dad say, "Put your worm on the hook."

I looked at Dad and begged him to put the worm on the hook for me. I remember coming up with all kinds of excuses: "I can't touch it; it's icky. Dad, my fingers will get slimy. Dad, what if it bites me?" I could tell that Dad was losing his patience, so I held the worm with my fingertips and closed my eyes.

Finally, Dad said, "Just give me the worm!" While Dad was putting the worm on my hook, I thought, "Closing of the eyes just might work for dreaded tasks."

After the worm incident, Dad taught me the step by step of how to cast a line. It wasn't too difficult. I only got the hook caught in a little bush, around a rock, on a branch, and on the canvas seat leg. Not too bad for a beginner.

Finally, both poles were in the water, and Dad and I relaxed. It was quiet for a while, until I said, "Dad, what's that sound?"

Dad replied, "You know the sounds of crickets."

I replied, "It sounds like a million of them! Where are they hiding?"

Dad just looked at me and said, "Everywhere."

"Dad, did you hear that? What is that sound?"

Dad once again looked at me and said, "It is probably a little animal running through the bushes."

I asked, "What kind of animal do you think it is? It doesn't sound little to me!"

Dad looked at me again and said, "Cindy, you have to be quiet! You'll scare the fish away!"

I was ready to ask another question, when suddenly, my pole started bobbing up and down. Dad told me to reel it in, just like he had taught me. I tried—I really, really tried—but something strange started to happen. I don't know; maybe a ghost took over my body, or maybe the icky worms put a spell on me. All I know was the fishing adventure had taken a new turn, and Dad would never be the same.

I looked at Dad as he kept telling me to reel

it in slowly, and then my feet started moving from right to left and then left to right. I tried to dig into the dirt to get a good footing when my right foot knocked over the icky can of worms. My body started twisting like Chubby Checker dancing his famous dance. Voices came out of my mouth that would surely scare the biggest fish as I tried to watch those slimy brown worms inching their way toward me as if they were racing and I was the finish line.

My line was coming closer and closer to the water's edge. I pulled the line a little more and screamed, "It's a snake! It's a big snake!" At that very moment, my hand mysteriously let go of the pole. I turned around and saw Dad just standing there, quiet as a mouse.

He finally looked down at me and said very calmly, "Cindy, that was not a snake. That was a little eel."

"But it looked like a really big snake," I said, still watching those pesky worms. I looked out over the river and wondered how that little eel that looked like a big snake could possibly swim and pull Dad's rod at the same time.

As we packed up the bag with the sandwiches, snacks, thermos of coffee, and the bottle of orange soda, I wondered what Dad was thinking. He was quiet as he put his pole, canvas seats, lantern, and the empty can that once held the icky worms in the back of his truck.

Soon, we were on our way home when Dad said, "Cindy, I don't think fishing is the right thing for you." I looked at Dad and thought for a moment, and then I replied, "I think you are right."

I told him I was sorry for losing his pole and accidentally kicking the worm can over. Then Dad smiled his special smile, and I knew that all was okay. I smiled because I would never have to touch those icky worms again!

Laughter for One
(Never Trust a Guinea Hen)

I grew up on a small farm in rural Pennsylvania. Our farm had a menagerie of animals from a few heifers to rabbits, pigs, chickens, and ducks. One day, our father brought home four guinea hens. They had thin necks, featherless heads, gray feathers with small white dots, and a strange call. In all honesty, they reminded me of vultures waiting for their next meals.

However, Dad thought they would be a good addition to our farm. He told us that they would warn us if anyone came into our yard. Dad compared them to a watchdog—you know, a dog that barks the first time he or she sniffs the smell of a person tiptoeing on your property. I looked at Dad as he explained how wonderful it was going to be knowing that we were protected by those hens. As a young teen, I thought to myself, "Really?" Mom never locked our doors when we went to bed, and our dog, Mickey, never barked while we were sleeping!

I think Dad just wanted to add to his collection of animals that roamed our farm. He could have at least brought something a little sweeter to look at and who didn't make the hair on your arms stand on end!

As the days went by, the guinea hens seemed

to settle into their environment, or at least I hoped so. Do you think that a guinea hen can sense when it is not liked? They always seemed to look at me a little differently than they looked at my sisters. It almost looked like they were smiling at everyone else but not at me. I tried my best to be kind to them. I truly loved all the animals on the farm—well, maybe not the rowdy roosters. But even those rabble-rousers didn't scare me like those guinea hens did. Then one day, everything changed.

The guinea hens started to walk around me without their heads hung low. I did not have the feeling of red darts flying out of their eyes, heading straight toward me. I started to relax. I started to like them. Well, just a little bit. When I fed them their dinner, it almost looked like they were doing a little jig. I smiled as I walked back to the house. They had finally accepted me. I felt good! Just maybe I'd make myself believe that they were cute. Not! I couldn't wait to tell Mom what happened. She would never believe that I was over my fear of the guinea hens.

Six squares of the sidewalks to go to reach the back door. Five squares of the sidewalks to go. Then it happened. I heard a sound that stopped me in my tracks. I thought someone had come into our yard. I turned slowly, and there they were, heads down, squawking, running, imaginary red darts shooting out of their eyes. I turned to run but felt like I had cement shoes on. I yelled for Mom and said to my feet, "Feet, please don't fail me now!" Oh no, the kittens were sitting by the back door. Not just one but at least five or six. I didn't want to hurt those little darlings, so I did the next best thing. At least I thought it was. I ran around the side of the house, past the outhouse by the huge pear tree laden with the sweetest fruit. I told myself, "Stop thinking about the juicy pears, and keep running! Mom! Help Me! Please!"

I kept running and then glanced back and realized that those hens were almost on my heels. I ran like the wind, but they kept chasing me. My heart was beating as I rounded the corner and saw Mom standing in the yard holding her dish towel. "Mom, help me!" I ran past her and then heard her yell for Dad. As I passed the pear tree again, I looked back and saw Mom, swatting at the hens with her towel, running as fast as she could. Around we went.

As I rounded the corner, there seemed to be more kittens sitting at the door. I thought, "Did they invite their friends?" I kept running, listening to Mom mumbling at the guinea hens as she ran faster. "Run, Mom, run!" Suddenly I heard Dad yell for us to stop. We stopped.

Dad got between us and those demons from

the barnyard. He looked at the guinea hens and shouted, "Get going," and go they did! They hustled when they heard his voice.

Mom and I stood in the yard sweating after our marathon as Dad got the hens a distance away from us. Mom asked Dad what took him so long to help us. He replied, "It's not every day you get to see a show without buying a ticket!"

Mom and I looked at Dad and said, "Very funny!" Then we headed into the house for something cold to drink. As I looked out the window, I could see the hens inching their way toward the house, and instantly the hair on my arms stood up. Soon after, the guinea hens were gone. Dad had found them a new home. As I thought of the new owners, all I had to say was, "Never trust a guinea hen!"

The Rabble-Rouser Rooster

I grew up on a small farm. Our farm was not a dairy farm or a horse farm but a farm with a menagerie of animals: rabbits, ducks, pigs, a few heifers, one bull, several cats, and a beagle named Mickey. Oh, I left out the dreaded chickens, a few possessed roosters, and three or four guinea hens that acted like terrorists. The first list of animals was sweet and cute and always brought a smile to my face; however, the second list scared the daylights out of me!

A Journey Down Memory Lane…

I remember begging Mom not to send me to the henhouse. She looked at me with her twinkly sky-blue eyes and straight face and listened as I gave my reasons for not collecting the eggs. As I remember, it went something like this:

"But, Mom, the chickens don't like me. They won't give up their eggs. The rooster pecks at my legs. And, Mom, you will never guess what that dumb red rooster did yesterday!"

Mom just stared at not me, not saying a word.

I continued, "Mom, that rooster started scratching the straw on the floor and then ran and flew high and landed right on top of my head!"

She kept looking at me and then said,

"Now, Cindy, they are just being chickens. Stop exaggerating about the rooster. He never bothers me. Now go do your chores!"

"But, Mom!"

"Go," replied Mom as I slowly walked out the door.

I took baby steps with my head hung low, dreading those chickens, when suddenly, I heard Mom laughing. "That Cindy—she sure does have an overactive imagination!" I sighed and thought, "I am not making it up; those chickens really do not like me!"

As I passed each cat and kitten, I shared my story about the wretched chickens. Suddenly, I heard a voice that made me pick up the speed.

"Cynthia! You have fifteen minutes to feed the chickens and collect the eggs!" It was Dad. I knew better than to dawdle. Then, as I quickly told the last cat my dreaded story, I had an idea.

The Plan…

I ran back into the house and swiped my mother's straw hat off the hook in the kitchen. It was the hat Mom wore when she worked in her garden. Then I ran up to the orchard and found a long stick, longer than my arm. I was ready!

As I entered the barn, I saw Dad feeding the heifers, so I bent over and quickly and quietly ran through the barn. However, I forgot that the back-barn door squeaked, and as I pushed it opened, all I heard was a crack and then a slam. Once again, I heard laughing. This time, it was Dad. I kept thinking, "What is it with all the laughing today?"

Please Say a Prayer for Me…

I would be brave. I was prepared. I would conquer the red rooster, and I would get those eggs! As I stood at the dreaded door, I took a deep breath, checked to see if my hat was on right, grabbed hold of the stick, and slowly opened the door. I walked in and scanned the room, and to my surprise, the alien red rooster was eating and not paying attention to me.

The hens seemed content sitting in their

boxes. I softly let out a breath and walked over to the first hen. I took my stick and very gently lifted her up just far enough to reach in and get her large white egg…when suddenly I realized that I had forgotten the egg basket.

I turned and went back out the door, opened the squeaky barn door, bent down, and quickly ran back through the barn, hoping Dad would not see me. As I approached the small white shed where we kept the egg basket, I remembered that Mom had taken it in the house.

I took Mom's straw hat off, put the stick by the door, and ran as fast as I could up the sidewalk. I opened the back door and stopped to see if my mother was in the kitchen. She wasn't there; however, I heard her beautiful voice singing one of her favorite songs. Mom was nearby. I dashed over to the sink, grabbed the basket, and flew out the back door. I ran back to the white shed, put on Mom's hat, grabbed the stick, stood by the door, checked to see where Dad was, heard him talking to Blackie (the bull), bent down, ran through the barn, and opened the squeaky door. Once again, I heard Dad laugh.

   I stood by the chicken coop door, caught my breath as I fixed the tan hat, held the stick, and opened the door very slowly. This time, the red rooster was nowhere to be found. I decided to start at the last hen box since the rooster was not there to bother me. I used my stick to raise the hen, and as that cackling white girl pecked at the wood, I grabbed her egg! That was easy! In fact, the rest of the hens cooperated very nicely. My hen stick really worked! Suddenly, I heard something familiar. As I turned around, there he was in all his glory, standing tall like a statue, right by the chicken door that led out to the barnyard.

I swallowed hard and slowly started walking over to the door. The rooster started scratching at the straw and then stopped and looked at me. I froze, and for a few seconds, it looked like we were having a staring contest—you know, like the contest to see who would laugh first. But I wasn't laughing. The rooster headed toward me, and before I knew it, he was on top of Mom's hat! His claws dug into the hat several times while I shook my head. Finally, he flew off, and I ran out the door. As I stood shaking, I took my mother's hat off, and there it was: the proof I needed.

I put my hat back on my head and this time walked with my head held high back through the barn. I put the basket of eggs in the shed and headed toward the house. Mom and Dad were having coffee as I walked into the kitchen. They both stopped and looked at me for a few minutes. I stood there and did not say a word.

The hat said it all!

Laughter for Two

The two stories you are about to read are true. The events leading up to the laughter really happened with the help of a little mouse and a secret leaking roof.

The Uninvited Visitor…

In the mid-sixties, my cousin LaRue came to live with us after her mother, my aunt Anna, passed. I was so excited and could not wait for her to arrive. Mom, Dad, and I worked hard to make the two storage rooms over the kitchen into a bedroom for the two of us. The rooms were not much by today's standards but were just right for two young teenage girls.

Finally, the day arrived, and I do know who

was more excited: LaRue or me. I could not wait to show her the room we would share. As we got to the top of the stairs, I slowly opened the small door and stepped in. I turned to LaRue, waving my arms to welcome her. I saw her eyes scan the heavy light-tan cardboard ceiling and wood and cement walls. She walked through the two small rooms; saw the older windows, one in each room; and then glanced down at the wide wood floors with the small worn carpets here and there.

LaRue smiled. "Wow! It's like we have our own little apartment." I was thrilled that she liked it! For months, we enjoyed our two rooms. We fixed the little apartment up with one room being our bedroom and the second room our living room, with a desk for schoolwork, two comfy chairs that Dad bought at an auction, and a small table. We even had a mirror hanging on the wall over the table.

LaRue and I had so much fun! We would tell secrets, giggle, and just be silly. And then it happened…

It was a cold winter's night. Mom had brought in extra blankets—three, to be exact. As we finished rolling our hair with the pink rollers that had hard pink coverings that snapped on, we grabbed our blue shower caps with little tiny flowers, covered our heads, jumped into bed, and waited for Mom to cover us to the point of looking like statues. We honestly wondered if we would ever move again! Mom laughed as she left the room. I remember her turning and mentioning that we were a sight for sore eyes. It should be noted that LaRue and I shared a full-sized bed. After sharing about our day at school, we fell asleep.

The next morning, I was the first one up. My cousin rolled over just as I put my housecoat on. I was just about ready to wake her up when something caught my eye. I thought I was dreaming at first. But as I took a second look, I left out a scream that woke LaRue up. She started screaming like a banshee before her feet hit the cold floor. Picture this: two girls, with rollers hanging from their heads, holding each other and screaming at the top of their lungs. Suddenly the small door opened, and in walked Mom, followed by Dad.

Mom said, "Girls, what's going on?" The only thing we could do was continue to scream as a roller or two flew across the room as we pointed to an oval gray shape with a tiny tail and little whiskers.

Mom look at Dad, and they both started to laugh. LaRue had slept on a mouse! After all the excitement, Dad removed the mouse. Of course, we decided not to even sit on the bed, wondering if the deceased little mouse had brought a friend.

The Secret Leaking Roof...

It was a rainy night, a windy night—a night my cousin LaRue and I would never forget. But let me start from the beginning...

A few days before the torrential rain and gusty winds, LaRue and I discovered a tiny little leak in the ceiling right above our bed. When I say tiny, I mean a drip every ten minutes or so. As we watched the drip, we decided that since we were teens—or should I say, barely teens—surely, we could figure out how to fix the hole without telling my parents.

As I remember, the conversation went something like this: "Do you think we can fix the hole?" asked LaRue.

"Maybe we could plug up the hole," I replied.

"I have some gum in my purse," said LaRue.

"It might work!" I exclaimed.
So LaRue got out of bed, walked to her purse, took out a piece of fruity gum, and started chewing. When it was ready, I stood on the bed and pushed the wet, sticky wad up into the tiny hole. It seemed to do the trick. So, we turned off the light and went to sleep.

During the night, LaRue woke me up and told me she had a wet foot. I turned on the light and noticed that the gum that we thought had solved our problem was on top of our blanket, which was getting wet. We looked at each other and thought for a while. Finally, LaRue said, "I have an idea. We could use the plastic bag from the cleaners to stop the leak."

I got out of bed and got the bag. LaRue and I folded the bag and then used tacks to attach it to the ceiling. I took the wet blanket off and put a dry one on us, and we both fell back to sleep.

LaRue woke up about an hour later and poked me on my shoulder. "Cindy, look up at the bag." I looked up and saw a bubble—not just a small bubble but a big one. We decided to watch it a little longer before we woke my folks up. Mistake! Before we knew it, the tacks flew from the ceiling, and the nicely folded bag loaded with water landed on our bed. We were soaked! We jumped out of bed and let out a scream. There we stood with our curlers half off our heads, in wet pajamas, looking at our wet bed. There was even water on the floor, and of course, water was still coming through the roof. When Mom opened the door, she could not believe what she saw. Although Mom and Dad were upset with us, they could not help but laugh. I remember hearing Mom say to Dad, "Those girls are two peas in pod!"

Yes, Mom, two wet peas in a pod!

Winter on the Farm

This morning as I looked out my window, I couldn't help but notice the huge piles of snow. It brought back so many memories of winter on the farm. I remember a time when the weatherman predicted snow flurries off and on during the day. Snow flurries indeed! We were snowed in for over a week!

My mother had done her weekly shopping a few days before the "snow flurries," so she felt as if we would be okay. It was a time when my father was ill, and Mom could only buy what we really needed.

She was always positive but stepped her smile up when times were lean. Mom would say things like, "We will be okay. We'll get through this." During the summer, Mom worked hard and canned a lot of fruits and vegetables. However, she also had a very kind heart and would help anyone who needed it. That was the case of the winter the snow flurries swirled like winds in a hurricane.

Mom came from a very large family, and that winter, with illnesses within her family and the loss of jobs, her kindness shone through even more. She would fix boxes up when there was a need. I remember her smiling as she said to one of my uncles, "Just a little something to hold you over." Mom's generosity meant our shelves were very low. But still Mom always looked on the bright side.

Four days into the mighty storm with the howling winds that curled your toes, we ran out of milk, bread, and Dad's medicine. Our road was not plowed, and things were starting to look a little bleak. I should mention because of the howling wind; the drifts grew steadily each hour.

Mom helped Dad carry coal up to the kitchen for the white stove, with one side being gas and the other coal or wood. That afternoon, my mother's sister called to check up on us. I believe Aunt Mae could hear through Mom's "We're okay" and realized that we were not.

My mother's sister put her husband, Uncle

Charlie, on the phone, and he asked Mom what we needed. She did not want to burden them, but my dear sweet uncle would not hear of it. Finally, Mom told him to just bring milk, bread, and Dad's medicine from the drug store.

Uncle Charlie told us to be at the end of our road in one hour. I should mention that our house was about half a mile from the main road. As sick as my dad was, he put on his boots, winter coat, hat, and gloves and got out the sled. I went along to help pull the sled back home. It was hard walking through the deep snow, but I loved it. Dad told me to slide my feet in the snow like he was doing to help make a path for on the way home.

We only had to wait a short time for my uncle. Dad and I could see his smile as he drove up. He carried three bags to the sled and helped Dad tie them to the sled. Dad mentioned that he thought Mom asked for just milk, bread, and his medicine. But sweet Uncle Charlie said, "Lee, you will need more than milk and bread to get through this storm." My heart melted despite the cold, snowy day.

When we got back to the house, we could not believe our eyes. Uncle Charlie not only bought the needed items but surprised us with some extra meat, potatoes, and canned vegetables. The biggest surprise came that evening when Mom poured us each a cup of milk and told us to close our eyes. When we opened them, right in front of us was the biggest bag of cookies we had ever seen.

That night when Uncle Charlie called, Mom thanked him for getting the extra things. Then she handed each one of us the phone, so we could thank our generous uncle for the cookies. His reply was simple: "You can't have a glass of milk without some cookies!"

We all looked forward to spring that year. Did I mention that at the bottom of one of the bags was a twenty-dollar bill to tide us over? Lesson learned from that winter: when we help others, generosity and kindness always find their way back.

Christmas on Ayers Road

It was Thanksgiving Day, and Dad was like a kid in a candy shop. Although he loved turkey with all the fixings, he loved what was right around the corner even more: Christmas. I could see the excitement building after the last bite of pumpkin pie was eaten and washed down with a gulp of coffee with just a splash of milk.

He looked at Mom, smiled his "it's time" smile, got up, put on his worn winter coat, and headed to the garage, where the plywood was waiting for him. Dad opened the faded white garage door and walked to the back; you could almost hear the wooden boards groan,

"Finally." Dad carried each board to the house while my mother held the kitchen screen door open for him. My two sisters, brother, and I scurried to the living room, where we watched with excitement as the first board found its temporary home on two wooden horses, evenly divided to keep the board steady.

We knew everything entering the blue room with the big white-flowered wallpaper would soon transform the room into a beautiful place. Soon the second board was in place and took on the shape of the letter "T." Dad never let on what shape the boards would take. After the shape was in place, Dad would go up to the attic and carry down the many boxes of trains.

My father started collecting trains as a boy and continued into his later years. After he married Mom, he would look for them at auctions. I must admit that Dad loved auctions. Sometimes, he would know someone who wanted to sell a piece or two of a train set. Mom would put aside a little money each payday and then surprise Dad with just enough to buy the piece. It was her way of showing her love and gratitude for a husband who worked hard at his job and who also helped our neighbors when they needed an extra hand around their farms.

My father, God love him, loved everything about trains, from the engines puffing smoke to the caboose bringing up the rear. He particularly liked the little plastic houses that made up small country towns. I remember the itsy-bitsy plastic people that Mom and I painted with a magnifying glass. The plastic people, I would give my eyeteeth to have today. I gave each plastic person I painted a name. Dad would laugh as I told Mom the name of each boy, girl, man, and woman.

I remember how much time Dad spent getting the "T" platform just the way he wanted it. It had to be ready in time for Christmas. Dad would work late into the night and then get up quite early in the morning for work and then start over again after dinner. He beamed when it was finished as we children stood in awe, looking at the homemade mountain Mom had made sitting in the corner of the table and leaning against the front door. Dad would push the lever on the control, and the train would huff and puff around the track, going through little towns and passing farms, and rushing past all the little tiny plastic people waiting for the train to stop.

Mom and Dad both loved Christmas. Although Mom would help Dad with the platform, decorating the rest of the room and getting the small real tree ready was her favorite thing to do. Dad always left room on the platform for the tree with the large, hot, bright bulbs; ornaments; and tinsel. The last thing Dad did to complete the platform was to tack corrugated chimney paper all around the bottom to hide the empty boxes. When everything was to Mom and Dad's liking, they would turn to us and ask us not to touch the fake dirt roads, move the people, or pick up any of the buildings. Being the oldest, I understood. However, my younger sisters and brother did not. Mom spent many a day fixing the roads, returning the plastic people and animals back to their homes, and reminding us not to touch.

Mom and Dad always made Christmas special for us with the bright lights, wonderful aromas coming from the kitchen, the red cellophane wreaths with the candles in the middle at the windows, and of course the stunning platform. Sometimes when I watched the train going around the track, under the bridges, and through the mountains, it made me feel like I was on a Christmas adventure. Standing next to my younger siblings and seeing their excitement, munching on a sugar cookie, and dreaming of Santa always brought joy to me.

My mother loved to sing—and what better time than Christmas to entertain us with holiday carols. I would sing along with her as we worked in the kitchen. I miss that. Family would visit when all the decorating and baking were completed, and the laughter, smiles, and eating commenced. Sometimes, it would snow, and our Christmas would be extra special.

Yes, Christmas on Ayers Road was filled with family, wide-eyed children, a real tree with the bright lights, and a train chugging along a small track. But more than that, it was about a mother and father who loved each other and passed that love to their four children, Cindy, Donna, Emma, and Lee. It was a love that reminded us each year of the real reason for Christmas: the birth of our savior, Jesus.

Part Two

Memories of Mom

Happy Birthday to Our Angel

This is not a sad story. On the contrary, it is a story filled with fond memories of a woman who loved her four children, grandchildren, great-grandchildren, family, friends, bingo, lottery tickets, music, going to the casino, singing, telling jokes, and making everyone laugh. But before the tears and the laughter, here's a little background information.

A Walk Down Memory Lane… (1947)

Mom was one of fifteen children born to Mary and Amzi Transue. Her father passed when Mom was twelve, leaving Grammy a widow for many years. Several years later, my grandmother decided that she would like to start dating and met a gentleman by the name of Charlie.

Mom did not particularly care for Charlie and decided she had to try to do everything in her power to persuade him to mosey on his way. Now, she had help in the shenanigans that followed. In fact, her brother Lloyd and his future bride, Helen, plotted with Mom to get him out of the picture.

The Three Musketeers...

One summer afternoon, Charlie arrived to pick up my grandmother for a date. He parked his car in front of the house and went inside to ask if his date was ready. From the side of the house came Mom, Uncle Lloyd, and Helen.

Uncle Lloyd and Mom looked around to make sure that Charlie was out of sight. Then Uncle Lloyd released the brake of Charlie's car while Helen jumped in and took over the steering wheel. The other two musketeers pushed Charlie's car down the street and parked it behind the ice plant. All three of the musketeers then walked back to the house and acted real sweet to the man they wanted to get rid of.

After a bit, Charlie got up and went outside to wait for my grandmother. She heard in a Pennsylvania Dutch accent, "Mary, Mary, someone took the car!"

Mom, with her sparkling blue eyes, answered in a serious voice and said, "Charlie, maybe some kids were fooling around and moved your car!" Charlie thought about it and then went out to look for his car as Mom, Uncle Lloyd, and Helen stood by the window, covering their mouths to muffle the laughter, and waited to see how long it would take for Charlie to find his car.

They had succeeded, at least for that night! But the escapades did not end there… One afternoon, Charlie came to take my grandmother out to lunch. When he arrived at the house, my mom snuck out the back door with something in her hand. She raced down the sidewalk and around Charlie's car. Then Mom knelt and shoved a potato up his exhaust pipe. He and Grammy got into the car and started down the street when suddenly, the potato flew out, and Charlie stopped the car. He jumped out of the car, raced around, opened my grandmother's door, and said, "Mary, someone shot at my car! Go and hide!" Mom stood laughing as Charlie drove quickly away.

Now there was a reason that Mom, Uncle Lloyd, and Helen did not like Charlie. It seemed that he was two-timing my grandmother, which led to the last "let's get Charlie out of the picture" prank.

It was a Friday night, and Mom saw Charlie pull up to the house. My grandmother did not want to go out with him, since she finally realized what he was up to, so Mom told her mother to stay in the closet until she came to get her. Charlie came to the door, and Mom told him that her mom was not at home. He did not believe her and stepped inside to see for himself. Since he didn't see her, he left. Mom walked out with him and then saw one of her friends. She sat outside for quite a time before she remembered her mom was in the closet. Although my grandmother was upset, she agreed it was worth it to get rid of a man who really did not care about her.

Over the Years…

Mom's humor continued over the years. When Dad was living, Mom would have her funny way making everyone around her laugh, and it did not matter where she was or what she was doing. She was great, and everyone loved her.

A Little Sadness…

Mom had her share of illnesses over the years—a brain tumor, several surgeries, and three strokes—but still her humor stayed strong. She worked hard to get her life back each time a mountain surged up. This beautiful woman, who lost so many of her family to mostly cancer, cried, grieved, and then used her humor to climb yet another mountain.

In the fall of 2013, our mother was diagnosed with a fast-growing mass in her stomach. We, her children, were told that she only had a few months, if that, to live. Since I was retired, Mom came to live with me. Hospice came once a week in the beginning as Mom adjusted to her new home. In the beginning, it was as if she wasn't sick at all, but as the weeks wore on, the changes were evident that her time with us was quickly coming to an end. Our hearts broke for the mother we loved so dearly.

Nightly Talks…

Although Mom was so sick, her humor was still there. Every evening, after everyone left for home, Mom and I would talk. They were great talks—talks that kept me going and still do. She reminded me of things that I had forgotten. We talked about our farm life, Christmas, and memories we had all made over the years. They were precious talks—loving talks sprinkled with laughs and joy.

Mom and the Pastor…

One day my pastor visited Mom. Although she had never met him before, she did not have any trouble breaking the ice. The following is a conversation Mom had with the pastor.

Mom: "You're really tall! How tall are you?"

The pastor: "I'm six feet five."

Sitting, watching, and listening, I held my breath. Mom's blue eyes were twinkling, and I could tell she was thinking.

Mom: "How tall is your wife?"

The pastor: "She is five feet two."

Mom: "Really?"

I knew it was coming! She was quiet, real quiet. I was holding my breath! It was coming; I just knew it.

And then Mom said, "How's that working for you in the bedroom?"

Without missing a beat, our pastor said, "Well, Roberta, I haven't had any complaints yet!"

They both laughed and laughed! So, did I!

On Her June 8 Birthday…

Happy Birthday, dear Mom! You taught us well. You loved us, took care of us, and taught us right from wrong. The lessons that Donna, Emma, Lee, and I learned are priceless. We thank you for filling our hearts with love for each other—a love that will always be there through thick and thin.

As I sing "Happy Birthday" to you, I can almost hear your laughter. Always remember, Mom, that you are forever in my heart. Your memory will live on and on until we meet again.

A Piece of My Heart

The following are a few journal entries written one month after Mom's death. It is my hope that my words will touch all those who may have lost a loved one.

January 13, 2014…

Mom, one month ago today, you passed from this world to a beautiful, love-filled home named heaven. I know you are enjoying your family and can only imagine the laughter, hugs, and kisses going on right now. The last four weeks have not been easy, but knowing you are with your family and our Lord makes my heart feel at ease. I keep going back to those last few days when your health declined rapidly. As I watched you sleep, I thought back to the day you came to stay with me. I was very nervous and prayed for strength.

I watched you struggle with your feelings. One day, during your nap, I heard you say, "No! No, I won't!" You were crying when you woke up. I remember kneeling by your bed and asking you what was wrong. You told me that your mother said she would be coming to bring you home soon. I kissed your cheek and told you that it was just a dream; a dream that happened each time you closed your eyes. You fought those dreams until one evening, after everyone had left and it was just you and me. You dozed off and then suddenly opened your eyes and pointed to the ceiling. I asked you what was happening.

You replied, "Don't you see them?" You then started to name many of your sisters and brothers, your mother and father, and my late husband, Lambert. You changed that day, Mom. There was calmness in your eyes and acceptance in your heart. As I began writing this entry, I decided to choose a word that expressed my feelings. I chose "grateful." I am grateful for your love. I am grateful that you kept me and did not give me up for adoption. I am grateful for all the wonderful things you taught me. I am grateful for your sparkly blue eyes and sense of humor. I am grateful for your love of music and passing that on to each of your children. I am grateful for my brother and sisters and for the love, compassion, and help that they always showed you. I am grateful for the many years I shared with you. But most of all, I am grateful for how you always encouraged me, cried with me, and sang with me in the last Christmas season of your life.

We all prayed for you to be healed. You prayed to be healed every day. I struggled to tell you that I believed that God answers one of three ways: "Yes," "Wait," and "No, I have something better planned for you." Mom, he did answer our prayers and yours. On December 13, 2013, his answer was "I have something better planned for you." He took you home to heaven, where there is no pain, no sadness, and no tears.

January 14, 2014...

I loved making your breakfast and reading parts of the newspaper to you. Your favorite part was the obituary page. Some days you knew one or two who passed, and some days they were strangers. In the beginning, you could get around with very little help. I think it made you feel good to have some independence. Donna and I took you to your apartment building to visit with friends. You smiled when you sat on your furniture and ate lunch at your table. We knew you enjoyed the visit but could see the sadness when we left.

You loved to tell silly stories to your nurse, Sara. I knew you were thinking, but *what* was anyone's guess. You were a hoot, and I miss your wit so much. I was brave, Mom. I had to be for Donna, Emma, and Lee. Today's word is "faith." I am trusting my faith to get me through this difficult time.

January 15, 2014…

It is a very rainy, dreary day. I miss you so much today but am more productive. You would want me to get on with my life no matter how hard it was. I thought about all the death you saw over the years. I cannot even imagine the tears you shed losing fourteen brothers and sisters, along with your parents. My heart breaks thinking about it. You were a very brave woman. I don't know if I would have been able to carry on, but you did.

You loved watching old game shows and played along with them. You made me laugh when the contestants did not know the answer, but you did. You had your friends laughing on the casino bus with your jokes about everything under the sun. I loved the faces you made when you tried an unfamiliar food. My word for today is "joy." You filled my life with bubbles of joy! Thank you!

January 16, 2014…

When I think back to my journey with you, Mom, tears often come to my eyes. I witnessed you walking well to not walking at all. I remember calling my brother and sisters in a panic when you started bleeding out of your mouth and nose—not just a little blood but so much that I had to get a little wastebasket. They all came to help me.

You had to go to the hospice unit for a few days. I will never forget the call late that night from the hospice doctor telling me that you only had a few days to live. I brought you home and stayed with you constantly. You died the following Friday. In fact, you died on Friday the thirteenth. Hospice prepared me for what I might see at your passing. They told me that you might have eyes opened wide, fists clenched, and mouth open.

The night before you died, I got in bed with you and read my prayers and sang Christmas hymns to you. Mom, when you passed, you had the sweetest smile on your face and a glow from your cheeks. I knew you had made it home to heaven. My word of the day is "strength." Strength to get up each day. Strength to always be there for Donna, Emma, and Lee, whom I love dearly. Strength to endure the loss for years to come.

A letter to my mother in heaven…

Dear Mom,

I have wanted to write you since you left, but I needed a little time. Today is May 13, 2014. I miss you so much! Hope you are enjoying your family in heaven. Please tell them that I miss them dearly. Mom, I really enjoyed taking care of you, and our time together will always have a special place in my heart. I know you protected me the night you died. You knew my heart would totally break in two if I heard your last breaths. So somehow you made sure that I went to sleep. A sleep that felt like someone knocked me out. A sleep that only lasted a few minutes. Just long enough for you to take your last breath. It was a labor of love to take care of you. I know that Donna, Emma, and Lee feel the same way. How blessed I am knowing that the angels were in my home and took you to meet Jesus. Thank you for being the most loving mother that God could have ever blessed me with. Until we meet again, I promise to dance, sing, and remember your sweet smile. Thank you for the beautiful cardinal sitting on the front-porch railing the morning after you took your precious journey. Don't worry about Donna, Emma, and Lee. You know me—I will always look after them.

Love always,

Cynthia Jean

My Heartfelt Thoughts…

Life is short. Love your family, make a difference, and be a ray of sunshine!

The Bear Who Brought Me Peace

This is a story that should have been written almost three and a half years ago. I guess the old saying "time really flies" is true. In the corner of my bedroom in front of the window sits an antique grandmother's rocking chair. On the chair reside three teddy bears. I love stuffed bears—in fact, many from my collection adorn their very own Christmas tree.

And this is where my story starts…

My heart broke the day Mom passed. Within seven weeks after being diagnosed with a fast-growing mass at the base of her stomach, she took her journey to heaven. She died a peaceful death with a smile that put our hearts at ease. The following days were filled with tears, the funeral, more tears, the luncheon, and more tears as we cleaned out her apartment.

Then something strange started to happen—something that was hard to believe and that took me a while to figure out. It was something that made me smile as I looked up to heaven and said, "Thank you!"

My question to you at this point is this: Do you believe that our loved ones send messages after they pass? I know that there will be some readers who might say, "I think she flipped her lid!" And some may say, "Wow, she has a vivid imagination." However, I am sure some might say, "Yes, I believe that loved ones send messages." I cannot speak for my readers. I can only speak for myself, and yes, I believe that our loved ones somehow, someway send messages to us. Love never dies. I believe in heaven, and I believe God works in mysterious ways. So, sit back and relax as I tell my story about the bear that brought me peace.

It was about two weeks after Mom passed when my husband, who had gone up to bed before me, mentioned that he had heard Christmas music in our bedroom. My reply to him was, "Our bedroom? That can't be. Maybe a car went by with Christmas music playing." He looked at me with that "maybe you're right" look and walked away.

However, that very night, snuggled in my bed, I heard what sounded like "Jingle Bells" playing somewhere. I listened for the sound of a car but did not hear a motor running. I even got out of bed and checked the window in the front of the house and the windows on the side of the house. No cars. When I returned to my room, it was silent. I thought to myself, "Girl, you have had too many Christmas cookies!"

Two hours later, I was awakened by the same song, a little muffled but recognizable. Once again, I got out of bed and checked to see if a car was outside my window. Once again, nothing. I thought, "What are the odds of hearing the same song twice in one night?" I tried to put it out of my head and went back to bed, sleeping with one eye open and one ear listening, ready for the next time. I can't tell you if "Jingle Bells" played again that night, since trying to stay awake was never something I had ever accomplished.

The next morning over coffee, I told my husband that I too had heard the music. I asked him what song he had heard, and he replied, "I'm not sure, but I think it was the one with a one-horse sleigh in it."

My mouth gaped open as I asked, "Could it be 'Jingle Bells'?"

He looked at me, snickered, and said, "Yep, it was 'Jingle Bells'!"

I was perplexed, and at that very moment, the detective came out of me. I almost wished I had a sleuth hat and a pretend pipe. Columbo would have nothing over me. I would get to the bottom of the "Jingle Bell" escapade one way or the other.

For the next few days and nights, neither of us heard the music. Then on Christmas night, as I walked up the stairs to my bedroom, I heard "Jingle Bells" again. I hurried up the last couple of steps, but the music stopped. I checked out the windows: no cars in sight. Then as I turned, I heard it again. As I walked into my bedroom, the sweet sound of Christmas was coming from my rocking chair. I walked over slowly and picked up the bear. The music stopped. I pressed his paw and heard "Jingle Bells" play. Chills ran up and down my back. I put the bear back down, stepped back, and just looked at the bears sitting so comfortably as if they were old friends.

I stepped forward and picked up the bear once again. This time, I shook the bear—nothing. Not even a squeak. Then I held him upside down; nothing. It was not until I squeezed his paw, and squeezed it hard, did the song play. I placed him among his friends and went downstairs to share the news with my husband. He couldn't believe that it had been the bear.

That night, I read for about an hour before turning off the light. The bear was quiet during this time. I remember glancing over for one more look, and then I turned off the light. As my mind tried to relax, I felt tears filling my eyes. It had been an emotional and busy day, with a house full of family, an evening with my sister my brother and their families, and a heavy heart from missing Mom. Suddenly, "Jingle Bells" filled the air. This time it did not sound muffled. This time, it filled every inch of the room. When it stopped, I squeezed his little paw, and the old-time favorite played again.

I gently put the bear back down and went to bed. As I lay there thinking about Mom, a thought came to my mind. I remembered sitting at my dining room table with her. She was working on a word search, and I was working on a Christmas project. I was also humming a holiday song. Mom told me to sing it. The song I sang was "Jingle Bells." She joined me, and together we sang the song like we did when I was a little girl. How odd that I heard the same song coming from a stuffed bear! The bear only played for me when I squeezed its paw. Then something strange happened. As I tossed and turned during the night, "Jingle Bells" played three more times.

That was the last time I heard the music. The bear never played it again. In fact, I find myself looking at the bear and wishing it would play. But it hasn't.

I believe that Mom sent me a message. I believe she was telling me that she had made it home and was okay. That Christmas night and the early morning of December 26, 2013, started a healing that continues to this day. Although I miss Mom very much, I have a special place in my heart for the little bear that brought me peace.

I decided to write this story for a reason. With all the sadness, hate, and anger in our country and world, I thought a story about a little bear that brought peace to a broken heart just might brighten hearts. Finally, I believe that our loved ones are always with us.

Remember—love never dies.

The Incredible Ethel

This is a story about a special gal who brings happiness every day. Just the sight of her makes me smile. I have known Ethel for about twelve years and consider her one of my dearest friends. So, bear with me as I tell you about my incredible friend…

Ethel is very shy. She doesn't say much, but the two of us have no problem communicating. I understand when she is happy and when she is sad. Three years ago, Ethel's brother died. Her heart was broken. Ethel moped around and did not have much of an appetite. She would pace around her home, expecting to see her brother sitting in his favorite chair, gazing at her as he often did.

I was always there for her, talking to her and telling her that everything would be okay. I felt her pain and told her I would always be her friend. In time, Ethel did feel better, and she slowly started enjoying all her favorite things.

Seven months later, I needed Ethel. Mom was diagnosed with a fast-growing mass. She was only given a few months, if that, to live. I wanted to take care of her. It was important to me that Mom would be in familiar surroundings, with those who loved and cherished her. So, with the help of hospice and my sisters and brother, Mom came to live with me. The first day was busy, as all the days to follow. Then something amazing happened on the very first night.

Mom was sitting on my love seat, when a special visitor appeared. My dear shy friend came for a visit. She walked into the front room and went straight to Mom. What a smile my sweet blue-eyed mother had on her face. Ethel did not visit very long, but the happiness she brought Mom was priceless.

The next evening, my sister and her husband came to visit, and once again, Ethel entered the room and greeted Mom first and then the others. She was really dealing with her shyness!

Each day brought new challenges for Mom.

She went from walking independently to needing assistance to get up from a chair. Each night, Ethel would visit her, and Mom would smile. As the weeks went on, Mom got increasingly worse. At night, after she was in bed, Ethel would sit with me. There was no need for words since I felt her unspoken love and support.

Ethel started coming and spending more time with Mom as the weeks went by. One day, Ethel sat on Mom's bed, not realizing it was an air mattress. When the bed adjusted itself to Ethel's weight, she jumped up and left the room. Mom and I tried not to laugh, but I must admit it was quite funny.

The next day, when Mom was sleeping, I heard her crying and went in to kneel by her bed, but somebody had beaten me to it. Ethel was already by her side, touching her hand as if to say, "It's okay. I am here." When I asked Mom why she was crying, her reply was that her mother had told her in her dream that she would be coming for her soon. As I got up to leave the room, I felt the tears streaming down my face. Ethel stayed with Mom for a while and then left the room.

Mom, who had never been afraid of anything, asked me to sit with her that night and to please keep the light on. Ethel sat with me, never leaving my side.

The Monday before Mom's passing, my home was bursting with family. Mom had stopped talking, and her organs were starting to shut down. My shy friend could not handle the number of people, so she sat upstairs where she could be close by but not feel overwhelmed. There was raw emotion that night, and tears of sorrow flowed. Then there was silence, and I could hear my dear sweet friend crying as she sat at the top of the stairs.

Each day brought major changes with Mom's health. When she managed to open her eyes, they were not the same. Mom's lips looked parched as I gave her water from an eyedropper, hoping it would help her, praying that the cool water would bring her comfort. The days flew by like the wind: Tuesday, Wednesday, Thursday…

When I woke up that Thursday morning, I thought Mom had mucus in her throat but soon realized that it was the death rattle. My dear sweet Ethel never left her side. My family came to say their good-byes. I knew they were struggling as much as I was. That night, as my sisters and families left, they kissed Mom good night. I believe in my heart they knew it would be the last kiss they would give her. My brother was the last to leave. As I stood looking down at my precious mother, I said a prayer that the angels would come soon and take her home to be with her family in heaven. Soon, it was just husband, Ethel, and me.

Ethel looked at me and then looked at Mom. Then suddenly, she looked at the ceiling. I watched her eyes move along the ceiling above Mom's bed. Something strange was happening. My dear friend got in bed with Mom. She put her head on Mom's chest and kept one eye on the ceiling. My wonderful mother died early the next morning. She had a loving smile on her face and closed eyes as if she were sleeping. As my family arrived on that very cold day, I noticed that Ethel was nowhere to be found. She had gone upstairs to escape the commotion that death brings. I called to Ethel to come down, but she would not budge.

Soon, the funeral director came to take Mom. I heard a high-pitched, sad cry coming from upstairs. It was Ethel. She had lost her dear friend.

My Heartfelt Thoughts…

I believe that family members come to take us home. I also believe in angels. Without a doubt, Ethel saw something that night, whether it was my grandmother or one of Mom's many deceased sister or brothers—or an angel or two. I see Ethel every day; she lives with me. She doesn't visit with anyone anymore, just Rick and me. She is still my best friend and is always with me.

This is the end of my story about the incredible Ethel, my sweet, adorable cat who never came out to see visitors but came out for Mom and my family. If I learned anything during that difficult time, it was to always tell our loved ones just how much they mean to us. My dear readers, life is precious. It is fragile; live each day loving and caring for family and friends. Reach out to help those in need, and remember a smile can go a long, long way.

A Phone Call, a Visit, and a Blue Butterfly

This story is quite different from any other story I have ever written. One of the events leading up to this story has stayed with me for almost twenty-two years, while the other two happened just recently. What I am about to tell you brings a smile to my face and fills my heart to the brim.

Question: Did you ever have a dream that stayed long after your night's sleep? I am not talking about a day or two but about years, months, and weeks—a dream that you can recall with 100 percent accuracy. A dream you wished would never end.

Twenty-two years ago, my first husband,

Lambert, died from a massive heart attack. He was fifty-one. I was devastated when he passed. My children and I went through all the motions and emotions: the viewing, the funeral, the luncheon, and an ocean of tears.

I remember holding his comb, breathing deeply, taking in the scent of each strand of hair. It is funny how a strand of hair can fill you with comfort. I would stand in our bedroom closet hugging his shirts, just like I always hugged him, yearning for his closeness. I sat in his favorite chair and drank my coffee from his cup, desperately wanting to feel his warmth. I needed him to be there with me to stop the hurt and tears. I wished there was a stairway to heaven. I would have gladly climbed it to bring him home to our family. Although my heart was broken, I knew that our four children were hurting beyond words too, and I did not know how to help them.

I often stood in the dark and cried out to him, not knowing if I could make it through another day. I found myself begging and pleading with God to let me hear my husband's voice one more time. I wanted to tell him everything I felt in my heart, but most of all, I wanted to be able to say, "I love you" one more time. I wanted to tell him that I would take care of our family and somehow carry on. I waited and prayed every day for a sign that he had made it to his new home in heaven. Then one month to the day of his death, I received an answer to my prayer.

I had a dream that connected me to my husband. In my dream, I was looking out my living-room window, waiting for him to pull his car into the driveway, when suddenly, the phone rang. I picked up the receiver and heard a familiar voice—the voice of my dear husband. The conversation went like this:

"Where are you? I miss you. When are you coming home?"

He said, "I can't come home anymore."

I continued, "But why can't you? I love you so much!"

I was crying when he said, "I can't come home. I love you. Now, don't you cry."

I quickly said good-bye as I heard a click; he was gone. Although the dream was sad and only lasted a minute or two, I believed it was the message I had been waiting for. I knew he had made it home to his new home in heaven. When I woke up the next morning, I had such a beautiful sense of peace—a peace that started the healing of my heart.

About a month ago, I dreamed that I was sleeping in my bed with my left hand hanging straight out over the edge. I felt a familiar hand holding my hand. I looked up and saw my mother looking down at me. She smiled. Her soft blue eyes looked right at me as she said, "Everything will be all right."

Just then, my father walked into my bedroom dressed like he used to in his green work pants, tan T shirt, and suspenders. As he stood by Mom, he echoed her sentiments: "Yes, everything will be all right."

I loved that dream because it gave me a chance to hear their voices, to see their faces, and to hold my mother's hand. Although I know they are in heaven with their parents and siblings, I miss them so much.

My heart is overflowing with love that continues to grow for my parents, who molded me into the woman I am today, who shared my hopes and dreams, and who always believed in me. Although my dream was short, the peace it brought me will last a very long time.

The third dream has me scratching my head. I was sitting in my brown recliner watching television when a blue butterfly flew by my head and landed on top of the curtain that covers my sliding glass door. It was the most beautiful shade of blue I had ever seen. The blue beauty then flew straight at me and attached itself to the center of my forehead. I felt its wings fluttering on my skin. Each time its wings touched my skin, I felt a relaxing sense of peace.

I can still see the blue butterfly when I close

my eyes. I can still feel the softness of its wings, which fluttered many times. I compared the softness to comfort, a comfort that dwells in my heart. The funny thing is that now blue butterflies are showing up everywhere: in magazines, on Facebook, and on stained-glass suncatchers. Every time I see a blue butterfly, the same comfort I felt in my dream meanders up and again fills my heart with peace.

My Heartfelt Thoughts…

Some may say that God sends messages to us through dreams to bring comfort at a time when we feel lost or perhaps to teach us a valuable lesson. Some may say that our daily activities can activate dreams. And then some may even say that because we think about our deceased loved ones so often, the chances of dreaming of them increase. For me, I believe the first choice. I believe that through my grief of losing my husband and helping my grown children grieve, I had lost my peace. Lambert left so suddenly that I did not have a chance to say good-bye. In my heart, that precious dream gave me the chance to say, "I love you, and good-bye." Saying those words, if only in a dream, brought me peace.

When I dreamed of Mom and Dad, I believe that God wanted me to know that everything was going to be okay. Since my parents reside in heaven, I believe the peace I felt was a lesson to help me understand that I cannot help everyone who needs me, but he can.

Although the blue butterfly itself has me stumped, I do believe the overwhelming peace I felt from his wings and feel to this day was the ribbon, so to speak, that tied the three dreams together.

So, dear reader, whether you find peace through a dream, your family, or nature, grasp it, and never let it go. The peace you feel will shine through like the gentle breeze, reaching all those you love and those you have yet to meet. Spread the peace and see what happens!

The Christmas Orange

It was 1927, two years before the Great Depression started in the United States. Although times were tough, no one could ever imagine the depth of what was to come.

But for Mary and Amzi Transue, June 8, 1927, was a good day—a day filled with hours of anticipation, pacing by Amzi, and Mary doing what all expectant mothers do when they are in labor. Soon, Amzi heard the cry of a newborn and hurried to Mary's side. He stood by the bed looking at his loving wife holding their little baby—a girl with tiny fingers and tiny toes.

Amzi called the rest of the family into the

bedroom to meet their new sister, Roberta Lorraine. Roberta was the fourteenth child born to Amzi and Mary. She had auburn hair with the sweetest blue eyes that looked like an icy-blue stream. This sweet little baby, watched over by her parents and older brothers and sisters, went through milestones, not realizing how tough life would soon be for her family.

The Great Depression began in 1929, the same year Richard Transue was born. Richard was the fifteenth child born to Mary and Amzi Transue. Roberta loved her little brother with her whole heart. She was often heard giggling as she gazed at him sleeping in his hand-carved wooden cradle, the same cradle she had slept in.

Mary's Heart…

Everything was changing rapidly when the stock market crashed. People lost their jobs, fear set in, and food became scarce. Although Mary and Amzi were worried, they had something more powerful than the change that was impacting their lives. That beautiful force that grew and grew was love—a love that kept the family together.

Mary grew most of what they ate, along with canning and storing for the winter months. But with a large family and a kind heart, Mary often found that the food did not stretch as far as she would have liked it to. However, that did not stop Mary from following her heart.

It was told that Mary and Amzi never turned anyone away who needed a meal. It didn't matter how bleak each day looked; they were grateful for what they had and wanted to help all who knocked on their door. Mary just put less on each plate, so their new friend would have something to eat. She would often add an extra potato just in case a family member or a stranger stopped by.

Soon it was Thanksgiving, and one of Roberta's older brothers hunted, shot, and brought home a huge turkey that would become a feast for their large family. As the family gathered around the long rectangular table surrounded by benches on both sides, the children bowed their heads as Amzi said a prayer. Although the Depression was getting worse, Mary and Amzi knew in their hearts that they had a lot to be thankful for as they looked at their children sitting around the table, laughing and enjoying the delicious meal.

The Christmas Orange…

November turned into December, with snow falling on the first day. Mary's thoughts turned to her family and Christmas. There was no money for gifts, and Mary felt sad. She sold eggs for extra money, but most of that went to put food on the table and to pay a little on their monthly bills.

Mary and Amzi gathered their children

around the table and explained that Christmas would be different this year, and they felt their hearts breaking until a spokesperson among the children said, "It's okay; we understand." It was not as if Santa ever brought a huge bag of gifts for the children. Usually, they would receive one small gift each. But not this year.

A few days before Christmas, the children decorated the freshly cut evergreen with popcorn and homemade ornaments. They each hung one of their better socks on the fireplace. Mary checked to make sure that each sock was hole-free. As she inspected the last sock, she overheard her younger children saying a little prayer: "Please, Jesus, remind Santa to stop at our house." Mary smiled as her heart broke a little more.

The day before Christmas, Mary and Amzi went to the market to buy some flour when something caught Mary's eye. She went over and talked with the owner for a few minutes and then turned to Amzi and smiled. As they hurried home, Mary felt lighthearted as she thought about Christmas.

The next morning, the children were up bright and early. They bounced down the steps and headed to the tree. Mary and Amzi sat as the children waited for their stockings to be handed out. The oldest child explained that everyone had to wait until each one had his or her stocking. Excitement filled the room. Finally, the stockings were given out, and the count started. One, two three…the children slipped their hands into their stockings, and each pulled out a perfectly round, delicious-smelling orange. Then they put their hands back in again and pulled out a candy cane. The children smiled and were happy. As they carefully peeled their oranges, they told their mother and father it was the best gift ever!

Mary and Amzi smiled as parents do and said, "Merry Christmas, children!" Then thirteen voices chorused together, "Merry Christmas, Mom and Dad!" Even little Roberta giggled and giggled as she held tightly to her candy cane. Baby Richard cooed in his mother's arms. Santa had not forgotten them.

My Heartfelt Thoughts…

Mary and Amzi Transue were my grandparents. I never met my grandfather but knew and loved my grandmother. Over the years and weeks leading up to her death, Mom shared the Christmas orange story with me. She told me about the socks hung by the fireplace and the many oranges she received growing up. During the Depression, oranges were expensive. When my grandmother spoke to the store owner, she asked if she could pay a little each week for the oranges. He said yes. He gave the candy canes to my grandmother at no charge. That was the beginning of the Christmas orange story that started so long ago. I hope you enjoyed this special Christmas story, a true story about a family filled with love.

    Merry Christmas!

Part Three

Stories from my Heart

What My Teapot Taught Me

This is a story about a teapot. It is not a teapot to boil water for a nice cup of hot tea or a decorative sit-on-the-shelf teapot. It is a beautiful pink teapot, not bright pink or fuchsia but more of a dusty rose. My teapot has an old-fashioned look, with little round openings below a flower design that circles the neck of the pot. This special teapot is electric with a small bulb that warms a little dish that holds a square-shaped piece of wax. As the wax melts, it fills the air with the most delicious scent that tantalizes you into thinking about sugar cookies.

I light the teapot every night. The glow from the opening gives off a light that shines in many directions. It warms my heart to see the tiny rays circling around the pot, bringing light where there was darkness.

I Am Not Judging…

Each day as I read my newspaper, watch the news on the television, and listen to the radio, I am reminded how different people are today. Although there are many kind and loving people, there seem to be just as many who appear to be lost. I am baffled at the hate some folks have in their hearts.

I struggle with the lack of respect and empathy toward anyone who is different. It breaks my heart when children and adults are bullied to the point where they debate suicide. Elder abuse is increasing. How sad for those older men and women who are made to endure pain and humiliation. Tears flow from my eyes when I think of the cruelty toward animals that happens each day. I could go on and on with the sorrow that so many feel daily, but I think I will end, allowing you to ponder what tugs at your heart.

My Teapot…

When I close my eyes, I envision the teapot symbolizing each one of us. The light from inside filters outside the little holes, lighting up an area surrounding the teapot. I believe the light represents our heart. The warmth of the light resembles love, a love we can share with all we meet daily. This love continues to cultivate our consciousness, which would hopefully lead to knowing right from wrong. The light stays with us throughout our lives, enabling us to form friendships, fall in love, marry and have children, work, play, grow old, and pass on to heaven with a sense that we somehow made a difference. I am not saying that life is always easy; in fact, at times it can be downright tough! But if your light is strong, it will help you weather whatever comes your way. Your light is like a beacon, always loving when you don't feel like loving and always ready to help those you may or may not feel like helping but help anyway. The wealth of love instills selflessness. Sometimes we may struggle with making choices but love usually leads us to do what is right.

Before I turn on the teapot, the holes are dark. The darkness represents those folks who have lost their way for many reasons: dysfunctional families, drugs, and gangs. Whatever the reason, maybe at some point, the light radiated from them, and maybe it did not. Maybe along the way, the hurt was too much to bear, and the darkness filled the space where the light once shone. The darkness becomes their beacon, and love struggles to get through.

Where light shines with hope; darkness grows with discontent, hate, selfishness, and greed. Through the darkness, the lost folks see no light, even though it is always present. Some feel powerful in the darkness; some build walls allowing very few people in. Most who are lost are lonely, and deep in my heart, a part of me believes they want to be loved. When you see someone who is lost, what is the first thing that comes to your mind?

Hope…

The definition of "hope" is "a feeling of expectation and desire for a certain thing to happen. I believe that everyone has the light in them—some more than others, some with just a hint, some still searching. My desire is that those lost folks will find hope someday and that they will shine like the illuminating light from my teapot. Those who break the law, hurt someone, or take a life need to face the consequences for the choices they have made. However, I will always pray that they will find the light that just might start a change. Those who are lost because of mental illness need our support, love, and encouragement to help find their light.

There will always be people who allow their light to shine through loving, helping, encouraging, and caring for whomever they meet. It is my hope that you will continue to shine, making a difference wherever you go. Maybe if more people reach out to help others in need, smile a little more, and welcome those they do not know, the light might just spread a little farther. We can only try and hope.

Those Who Serve, Those Who Wait

On Saturday, February sixth, my husband and I traveled to the US Naval Academy with my daughter, her husband, and her father-in-law. We were on our way to watch my grandson Midshipman Christian Correale compete against army in gymnastics.

Now, I could write about how beautiful the academy is, how the navy beat the army, and how my grandson scored his personal best on the parallel bars and rings, but I'm not. Instead I choose to write about the parents of those wonderful young men and women who chose to serve their country, whether through the academy or enlisting in one of the military branches.

It has been my pleasure to visit both the US Naval Academy and West Point. I also have many friends who have a son or daughter serving at home or abroad. My oldest son enlisted right out of high school in the eighties as well. Whenever I travel and see a man or woman, regardless of age, dressed in his or her uniform, I always try to strike up a conversation. It is important to let our soldiers know how much I appreciate what they do not only for me but for all of us.

Whether I am at a military football game or gymnastics meet or talking with parents who have a son or daughter serving, I am always in awe of the tremendous love and pride they feel for their loved ones. It is written on their faces and heard through their beautiful words of love.

These amazing parents worry about their sons and daughters every day but continue to support them through letters filled with what is happening at home and encouragement. And somewhere within the body of words, they tell them how proud they are of their accomplishments.

They send packages filled with home-baked cookies, candy bars, and anything their soldier needs. Communication is the key to helping families cope with missing each other. I could go on and on about the feelings parents experience, the fear they feel, and the patience they practice every day waiting to hear, "I am coming home!"

One mother shared with me that she starts her day with a prayer for her daughter and all those who are serving. The prayer continues throughout the day and ends when she climbs into bed. This precious mother touched my heart.

A Father's Prayer…

It was dark when we started home from the academy. Before we left the yard, my son-in-law pulled over and got out of the SUV. I thought maybe the hatch opened, but instead, I saw him walk over to the water. My daughter shared that on every visit and before they leave, this sweet, wonderful father spends time in prayer. He prays for his military sons. He prays for all those young men and women at the academy, and he prays for peace. I must admit: tears meandered down my cheeks.

My Heartfelt Feelings…

As I finish this story, my heart is full of gratitude for the men and women who are serving our great country. I also think of the thousands and thousands who have served over the years. There are not and never will be enough ways to say thank you for the sacrifices these men and women have made and will continue to make. Because of their sacrifices, I have hope for the future—a future filled with peace. Please say a prayer for our military men and women and their families.

Minestrone for the Heart

Minestrone is an Italian soup filled with a variety of vegetables and ditalini noodles. Some like to add meat as well to this delicious soup. You can order it any Italian restaurant or make it at home. It is great served with crusty bread and a glass of your favorite wine. *Delizioso*!

This is where the minestrone ends, and the real story begins. Did you ever meet a family who invited you into their home and made you feel like you belonged? This is a story about Kathy and Rick; their golden retriever, Boo; Daisy the cat; their family; and a small house filled with love in every nook and cranny.

The setting: three cars driving in the rain

toward our destination. The first car held Pat and Jane leading the way. Next came my sister Donna and her husband, Albert, followed by my husband, Rick, and me.

I was always amazed by the amount of traffic and the busyness of this quite populated area; however, it did not stop me from turning my head and checking out the different styles of homes along the way.

As we turned into the driveway, I was taken aback by the charming house I saw before me. It was not a big house, but a lovely smaller home filled with charm. Little did I know what waited for me inside. After entering through the back door, I immediately felt embraced by the warmth of the dining room—you know, a warm feeling that relaxes you. A place where you can be yourself, be part of the conversations, and laugh like there is no tomorrow.

Pat Bruno, patriarch of the family, took me on a tour of the lovely house. As we started our tour, I noticed that each room had its own character. Warmth radiated from the walls, with pictures of a happy family with a few pictures of Pat's son, Kathy, and Joe's brother, who died of cancer at the young age of twenty-three.

The wall in Pat's bedroom held a part of his family all together in one room: laughing faces, memories of the past in pictures, and a painting from a son gone too soon. Still the love and warmth radiated from the walls, filling the hearts of all who entered.

Soon, I met Daisy the cat, whose sweet meow and presence commanded, "Look at me. I need my throat rubbed." Since I am an animal lover, I was more than happy to oblige. Boo, a very handsome male golden retriever, was friendly and welcomed everyone with a personal eye-to-eye "Hello!" Those two precious pets added to the warmth of each room they visited.

Then like a caravan, the rest of the family arrived, bringing food and more food. As each member came in and put a dish on the table, the hugging began. The outstretched arms did not end until everyone in the room was greeted. How refreshing to see the genuine love each one had for the other.

I found myself looking around the room, listening to the loving conversations and the laughter coming from the kitchen. One could almost hear the little house sighing a sigh of happiness.

Everything was ready. Hungry family and friends lined up, and the plate filling began. Some sat at the two tables in the dining room with the many windows; some sat in the living room with the cozy fireplace, plates loaded with delectable food and breathing in the most unbelievable aromas. Two prayers and an

"Amen" in unison were followed by the sound of knives cutting and forks swiping the plates as the eating commenced.

I sat in the corner of the added table in the dining room and listened to the conversations, watching the children having fun as they ate their corndogs and fried chicken. Even the beautiful baby girl with the high pigtails stole the show and had everyone in the palm of her hand with her infectious smile. I could not help but smile as I glanced at faces filled with happiness, enjoying each other's company and happy to be together.

Since I had recently had surgery, I was unable to eat any of the food that smelled so wonderful. However, Kathy, whose heart is bigger than a box of Valentine's Day chocolates, had made me things that I could eat. Thank you, dear Kathy.

As I continued listening and looking around, I wondered how many families were blessed to have members who genuinely loved each other, who helped each other, who laughed together, and who were always ready to lend a hand. What family would have a great-grandson pay tribute to his great-grandfather with a beautiful school report? The character of each person stood out to me on that rainy, damp day.

After the desserts were dished out, I asked if

I could help clean up and smiled when Kathy said, "Oh no, wait until it is almost time for some of them to leave. It's like magic. It will look like we never had anything." She was right! Everything was cleaned up and put away. How nice! As the families packed up and got ready to head home, the hugging started again along with "I love you."

As we got ready to leave, I looked around the house one more time. It had been a wonderful day with wonderful people who worked hard, cared about everyone they met, and always left a lasting memory for all to take home and hold in their hearts.

Riding home, I thought about a scripture

that encompassed the day. I felt in my heart that this was appropriate for the little house that held a special family.

"Love is patient and kind; love does not envy or boast; it is not arrogant or rude. It does not insist on its own way; it is not irritable or resentful; it does not rejoice at wrongdoing but rejoices with the truth. Love bears all things, believes all things, hopes all things, endures all things" (1 Cor. 12: 4–7).

In this time of uncertainty, it is so refreshing to be part of a family who shines. Thank you to Kathy, Rick, Pat, Jane, and the entire family for lessons from your loving hearts.

The Look of Not Knowing

We all have had days when we forget where we put our keys or a name of a family or friend. Some of us may forget the day of the week or a special occasion. I must admit that I am one of those people. Sometimes I have the look of not knowing more than I would like. It usually happens if I am stressed or tired or on information overload. It happens to many of us, especially as we age, but if we give ourselves a little time and try not to get frustrated, the information we struggled to remember will often meander back into our memories. However, there is much more to the look of "not knowing" than the hiccup of a slightly sluggish memory.

This is a story about three beautiful, loving women, two who reside in heaven and one who lives in a senior-care facility near my home. It is a story about a journey of hope, compassion, empathy, and patience. It is a story written from my heart for all those living or who have passed from dementia or Alzheimer's disease and their loving families who deal with losing them a little each day.

Millie…

She is small in stature, with brown eyes and hair, dressed in a coordinated outfit with stylish jewelry adorning her wrists, neck, and ears—plus, she wears a wonderful smile that could light up a room with an instant welcome: "It's so nice to see you!" Millie is a ninety-year-old senior who was diagnosed with pulmonary dementia a few years ago. For many years, Millie was able to live independently, but as time marched on, she started to have the look of "not knowing." Starting with little things at first and then along with a few health issues, independence slowly became more difficult for this precious woman. Since staying in her own home was not an option, her family had some decisions to make to keep their mother safe, while allowing her to be independent as she could be. Together, they decided that a senior-care facility would be the right option for a mother they loved so dearly.

As it turned out, Millie moved to a facility within walking distance of my home. In the beginning, accepting her new home was a little difficult, but soon she felt comfortable and enjoyed many of the activities of the day. Millie made friends easily and even enjoyed dinning with the "girls." I loved to visit her when I took my nightly walks. Millie always knew me. She warmed my heart, and I loved listening to her Italian accent. Millie always offered me a beverage and a sweet.

As time went by, Millie's dementia worsened; she started living more in the past and reverting to her parents and time in Italy.

She also needed a walker to help her with her unsteadiness. I remember one-time walking in and hearing her voice. I followed the familiar accent and found her chatting with one of the girls. They were sitting in the hallway on very nice-looking, comfortable chairs. She looked up and smiled and introduced me to her friend. After a few minutes, her friend left, and Millie wanted to go back to her room. She got up from the brown recliner and started to walk, but something was missing—her walker.

I said to her, "Millie, you forgot your walker."

She turned and said, "It's not my walker; it's yours." Millie would not take the walker, so

I followed close behind her, pushing my supposed walker back to her room. Lucky for us we were not far from her door!

I loved my visits but soon noticed changes in Millie. She always knew my name, and her smile was the same. However, after the initial hello, Millie would start talking in her native language of Italian. At first, I would tell her that I did not understand Italian, and she would stop and talk in English. But a few words later, she went back to Italian. I would just smile and move my head as if I understood every word. It was important to me not to offend this sweet, dear woman in any way. I love Millie—always have and always will.

When my mother passed, Millie had a kind word and hugged me tightly. When I would see her at picnics, we would sit and have great conversations. She made me laugh when I would visit her and always offered some candy or a treat. In the evening, Millie would keep an eye on the window, checking to see if the darkness was falling, and she would remind me to be safe when I would kiss her lightly on the cheek and headed out the door. Every time I left her room, I would hear, "Come again."

I plan on visiting Millie soon. I am hoping she will remember me. I think she will. Just a thought—wouldn't it be wonderful if what the mind does not remember, the heart does? I choose to believe that Millie's heart is so full of memories that it is overflowing.

Louella...

Louella was tiny in stature, with nicely done reddish hair, a raspy voice, blue eyes that looked like the sky, and a sparkly necklace that always complemented her outfit. She was always ready to lend a helping hand and was often seen standing on her porch roof washing her upstairs windows. Louella was my aunt. She was one of fifteen children. I loved her. There wasn't anything I wouldn't do for her. Aunt Louella had her illnesses over the years, including throat cancer, which explained the raspy voice. My mother and Aunt Louella were very close. They both enjoyed taking day trips to the casinos and always came back with the best stories.

Then something changed. Mom was a little hesitant to ask her to go on the bus. It seems that Aunt Louella was starting to roam and often could not be found. Then the look of "not knowing" started to show up regularly and stay longer and longer each time. I would talk to my aunt on the phone, and yes, I noticed some change, but it was not until I volunteered to pick her up and bring her to our family reunion that I got the whole picture.

It was a warm August day as I knocked on her door. She did not come right at first. In fact,

Aunt Louella peered out the oversized window next to her front door. She looked right at me but did not come to the door. I knocked some more and kept knocking until she opened the door. The look of not knowing gave me chills when she just stood and looked at me, seemingly lost in the moment. The conversation went like this:

"Hi, Aunt Louella. It's me, Cindy. I am here to take you to our reunion."

She looked at me for a few seconds and then smiled and said, "Oh, Cindy, it's you." My aunt was dressed in her nightgown and housecoat. She turned around and headed to the kitchen with record speed. Aunt Louella did not say a word but went right to work, stirring her boiling pots on the stove. Quickly, she spun around, looked at me, and said, "Why are you here? I must get the salads made for the reunion. My family will be here soon. Why are you here?"

I looked at her and explained that her family could not make the reunion this year and that I would be taking her to the reunion. I reminded her that she would be sitting at our table and eating with us. The look of not knowing took over, and she just could not understand where her family was. I must say that I choked back a few tears as I saw the confusion on her face. Aunt Louella was quiet as she stood stirring her macaroni. Then she turned and said, "I am sorry; I guess I forgot. I'll get dressed if you finish cooking for me."

As she walked through the dining room and climbed the steps, I heard her crying. We got to the reunion late that day, and even though my dear sweet aunt smiled, I knew her heart was hurting. After the reunion, as I drove her home, she shared that sometimes she forgot things and that she was afraid. As I walked her into the house, she turned and just cried and cried. I could see the fear in her eyes. The look of not knowing she experienced more and more each day not only broke her heart but left a hole in mine.

As I drove home, I decided that I would

call her family and fill them in on what their dear mother had experienced that day. It seems they were aware of a few memory issues but did not realize the depth of the not knowing. Soon after, Aunt Louella moved in with her daughter and stayed with her until her death. She was eighty years old.

Aunt Louella had Alzheimer's disease. When I think back to my loving aunt who was always cleaning or cooking, I smile because she was a gem—a beautiful gem ready to help anyone who needed help. A gem who loved her family and left volumes of memories. A gem who tickled my heart.

Roberta…

Roberta was small in stature, with eyes of blue that sparkled like diamonds. She loved to be comfortable in everyday clothes, sneakers, and socks; loved casinos and lottery tickets; and could play many instruments by ear. Roberta love to tell jokes and had many friends. She was kind and loving but a rascal at heart. Her family would look at her and hold their breath when the jokes started, not knowing what would be coming out of her mouth. Roberta loved to sing and compared herself to Sophia of the *Golden Girls*.

The woman I just described has a special name: Mom. Yes, Roberta was my mother. She was a mother to my sisters, Donna and Emma, and my brother, Lee. There is so much I could say about this precious woman whom I love even though she now resides in heaven. In 2010, Mom had a series of bad strokes; however, she persevered with the help of some physical therapy and was almost as good as new. Because of the strokes, Mom developed pulmonary dementia. The look of not knowing appeared more often than before the strokes; however, it did not get out of hand partly because of a more serious illness that took her life in 2013. I included Mom because I loved her and miss her so much.

Mountains to Climb

Beautiful mountains laced with trees

hide the tears that no one sees.

Mountains tall, mountains small,

mountains hiding the pain of all.

Everyone climbs a mountain each day,

feeling stress, fears, and loss and led

astray.

Don't forget the dreams that meander,

like a stream tickling our souls, waiting

patiently to play the role.

Take one step and then another; the

mountain reaches out like a mother.

Fear not your steps forward and back,

forward and back.

The mountain stands strong, cheering you on.

"Don't give up!" the mountain chants.

"The top is near; do not fear. Just persevere!

Step by step, forward and back.

Stumble easy; stumble hard.

Forward and back, forward and back."

Soon, bright sunlight warms the way.

The climb is complete; gone is the gray.

The mountain is happy as the trees sway, clapping their leaves as if to say, "You did not give up; you gave

it your all. Believe in yourself.
Believe in your heart.
Always remember each day is a
new start."

When I think of my life, I think of the many mountains I climbed along the way. Sometimes I felt like I was climbing daily. Often, I climbed small mountains, reaching the top in no time at all, while sometimes the tall mountains kept me climbing for days. Then there are the mountains that keep me climbing and climbing. I am still praying and hoping to reach the top at some point in my lifetime.

We will each have a mountain or two to

climb at some point in our lives. Some will have more than their share to climb; some will struggle with the climb, giving up before they reach the top, while others avoid the climb entirely.

I believe that one of the many keys to working through our hurts, losses, and problems of all sorts is to never give up. I realize that it is not always easy to move forward, make changes, solve problems, and heal broken hearts. But we must try and keep trying. I believe that everything that happens in our life happens at the right moment. And often than not, issues we are facing work themselves out with time and perseverance.

I think of the mountain as the problems we face in our daily lives, the dreams we dream, and the love and acceptance we are all looking for. When you are struggling with worry, pain, stress, and loss or trying to follow a dream, be brave and courageous! Be willing to take a leap of faith as you take each step to the very top of your mountain. The journey may take a while, but the end results will be worth it! Believe in yourself and start to climb!

On the Wings of a Cardinal

I love birds! All types of birds: red-breasted robins, purple finches, blue jays, doves, and even pigeons. However, my favorite bird is the cardinal. I love the brilliant red of the male and the reddish-gold color of the female. I love their heavenly sound as they sing their beautiful songs.

Just a Few Facts

- Cardinals have a life-span of up to fifteen years.

- They are monogamous, with the male often feeding his mate, beak to beak.

- Both male and female cardinals sing a precious song that is easy to recognize.

- The male's brilliant-red color is very similar to the red vestments worn by the cardinals of the Catholic Church, which earned this spectacular bird its name.

This is where my story starts; it is a little different from most of my work. It is a good story—a story from my heart and one that hopefully will fill your heart with faith, hope, and love.

Once upon a time, God created many different types of birds: large birds, medium birds, and tiny birds with long thin beaks. God in his wisdom painted each group of birds with pretty colors so they would be unique and easy to identify.

He gave each bird its own special song and taught them to sing in harmony, how to make a nest, and how to look for food. Then God taught them how to spread their wings and fly throughout the sky. After he blessed each bird, they made their way to their destinations to start their new lives.

God was happy with his birds, but something was missing. He kept thinking about all the souls that made their journey to their new home in heaven. God saw the happy souls as they entered their new, and he was happy.

However, he knew those left behind had broken hearts. He understood their grief and wanted to help them find peace as their hearts mended.

He thought about all the birds he had created, and one came to mind—one that would make a special trip to help God complete his plan. He called on his messenger, a symbol of peace and love—his white dove. God invited the dove to sit on his shoulder as he started his new creation.

First, God made a small plain bird about the size of a robin. Then he picked up his palette and studied each hue. He thought about the green like his trees, blue like his sky, and yellow like his sun. The white dove cooed as God carefully studied each color, waiting patiently for his Father to make just the right choice.

God smiled and chose red, like the love that filled his heart for all his children. He gave the redbird a crest and a black mask that encircled his eyes and stretched down to the top of his chest.

He told his dove to fly and spread the news that the redbird was finished. God could hear the birds singing their praises as they waited to meet the newest bird. God stood and admired his handiwork and then held the bird in the palm of his hand. He raised his creation to his mouth and whispered a special message ever so softly.

Then God held his hand up, and the beautiful redbird flapped his wings and flew off to fulfill his assignments. As the bird flew, he looked for a special tree, an evergreen, where he would wait for a whisper from above, a whisper that would lead him to someone whose heart was breaking. Someone who needed a special message.

Some believe that our loved ones who live in heaven send a cardinal to let us know they are thinking of us. I believe…

Mom passed away on December 13, 2013. Before her passing, she told me to look for a cardinal. She smiled her precious smile and stopped talking two days later.

The day she passed was the saddest day of my life. My brother, two sisters, and I hugged each other as tears streamed down our cheeks. We were devastated.

I remember waiting for hospice to come and remove her bed and equipment as I thanked God for his precious gift to our family. I also thanked him for the time he gave me at the end with this beautiful woman, who was my hero. Sleep did not find me on that cold winter's night.

The next morning, I pulled back my lace curtains in the room where Mom had passed, and I could not believe my eyes. There in all his glory sat the fattest, reddest cardinal I had ever seen. He sat on the railing of the front porch for a long time looking toward the window. I believed he was looking at me.

I found myself smiling as tears filled my eyes. In my heart I knew that Mom had found her way home. She had kept her promise. Something wonderful happened to me on that very special day. Although my heart was breaking, peace started to fill my soul—a peace that would carry me through the hard days and that gave me hope.

The cardinals seem to come for a visit when I am overwhelmed, missing Mom, or when I am not feeling well. They have even come on special occasions. Two swooped right in front of me on my last birthday. Maybe Mom and Dad both came by to say hello!

I know that some folks probably do not share my feelings on cardinals or my beliefs, and that is okay. Everyone has the right to choose in what he or she believes. However, after a loss that literally breaks your heart, seeing a cardinal just might put a smile on your face and tickle your heart. Even if you do not believe, the beauty of the cardinal speaks for itself.

It is my hope that all who read this will reach out to those who have lost a loved one, those who are going through a difficult time, those who are lost, and those who need a friend. As the cardinal soars from his evergreen to bring us a message, reach out, and bring your own message of love to all.

L'amour est la réponse

Six months ago, I took a nasty fall. However, being stubborn, I thought resting my leg, along with icing my knee a few times a day, would solve the problem. It seemed to help until I took another fall two months later the on the same knee. Once again, I tried to heal myself, but this time, the pain was too much to bear.

And the Doctor Shook Her Head…

Dr. Ann shook her head as she asked me why I waited so long to come in to see her. I told her that I did not think it was bad enough and did not want to take her time from someone who really needed her. She gave me her best doctor look as she wrote a script for an x-ray.

After we got the results, a decision was made that involved physical therapy. So, with script in hand, I entered the rehabilitation center, ready to work hard to get my mobility back.

Two Rays of Sunshine Entered the Room...

About two weeks ago, I heard a gentleman talking with a beautiful accent. He was warming up on the stationary bike while I was working on a series of exercises. Although he was out of sight, his voice meandered almost as if it was floating from the bike to my ears. I was intrigued.

Soon, he walked slowly into the main

therapy room holding on to his cane. He was an older gentleman with wavy white hair and crisp-blue eyes that reminded me of clear Caribbean water. To his side stood a lovely lady, his wife, holding on to his arm.

She was tall with chestnut-brown hair beautifully braided around her head. This lovely woman wore a long brown skirt and a white peasant blouse tied with a perfect bow. My eyes went to her vest, which was hand sewn with the most gorgeous embroidered designs on the lapels. Her outfit was complete with white stockings and dark-brown ballerina shoes.

This lovely lady smiled at everyone and said hello with the same accent that made my heat skip a beat. It honestly felt like the sun was shining on me, even though it was pouring outside.

As she took a seat next to her husband, they smiled at each other and then waited for the therapist to explain and demonstrate the exercise. She listened attentively and then spoke to her husband in French, smiled, and then started counting backward from ten to one very slowly: *dix, neuf, huit, sept, sexe, cinq, quatre, trois, deux, un*. This sweet vision counted for each exercise, making sure that her husband held the position for the desired time. In fact, she counted so much that I now know how to count to ten and back in French!

Although the gentleman struggled at times, he responded to his wife's encouragement. When he was finished, he looked at his wife and said, "I love you" in German: "*Ich liebe dich.*" He looked at the therapist and explained that he and his wife spoke six different languages!

The Magic of the Afternoon...

As the afternoon wore on, I listened as the woman with the beautiful accent continued encouraging and counting in French, with her husband counting back to her in Italian or Spanish.

They both giggled as they switched back and forth with different languages, trying to confuse the other. It was so sweet to watch the magic between them. Their love reminded me of a rainbow with its many beautiful colors arching high in the sky, where the pot of gold is filled to the brim with two hearts entwined to make one.

Before long, her husband completed his therapy and headed to the bathroom to change his clothes. His wife went in to help him dress. As I was putting my sneakers on, I heard their voices once again, this time coming back to wish everyone a good day.

I smiled as I looked up and saw this loving couple who had made a big impression on me—he in his nifty suit and tie, and she with her beautiful smile. He looked at me, lifted his hat, and placed it on his head. They wished everyone a good day and then together, arm in arm, walked out the door.

Although it has been two weeks, I still think of the beautiful woman with the warm smile and her outgoing husband, who filled my heart with the languages of love.

My Heartfelt Thoughts…

I never found out the names of the man and woman who touched my heart that day, but they sure taught me an important lesson. The lesson was love, pure and simple.

Dear Readers,

Love can change anything and everything. I

believe we all need to keep loving, whether it is our spouses, our children, our family, our neighbors, those we find difficult to love, or those we have yet to meet. When we have love in our hearts, we have hope. Be the pot of gold at the end of the rainbow. You might just change a life. Love is the answer!

Meatballs Filled with Love

When I think of meatballs, I immediately think of the ingredients it takes to make the tastiest meal that anyone could imagine. But there is more to it than that—much more. I am sure that just about anyone could make good meatballs, but it takes a special person and a lot of love to make them taste as if they were heaven sent.

This is a story about a special lady who radiates love wherever she goes. Her delicious meatballs and sauce put smiles on the faces of those who are lucky to enjoy them. A few years ago, I was introduced to a woman named Kathy. I knew from the very moment I saw her twinkly eyes and heard her kind voice that she was someone very special. Since that introduction, my respect, admiration, and love have grown for her. But it wasn't until I dined on her meatballs and sauce that I truly saw the angel that she is.

Picture this: a gathering of family and friends at my sister's home and food—lots of food—just waiting for everyone to dig into and enjoy. Then in come the meatballs and sauce. Everyone in unison sighs and looks up to see who is carrying the dish. It is Kathy with her smile and her "How are you? You look great!" This sweet, gentle woman can warm the coldest of winter nights with her smile and her words:

"What can I do to help?" Then the hugs begin with a positive little message for all those who see her outstretched arms coming toward them.

As everyone gets in line, Kathy meanders around, making sure everyone has everything needed. She then fills her plate and settles in among the others listening to the conversation. Those who have her meatballs tell her how wonderful they are and ask her to bring them again. Her answer is always "Sure, I would be happy to."

The conversations around the table and those sitting in my sister's living room are buzzing—not the kind of buzzing that hurts your ears but the kind that is warm and inviting with a sprinkle of laughter. Kathy makes it a point to converse with everyone. Listening from the kitchen, I can feel a cloud of caring floating throughout the rooms. The cloud of caring and love blocks out all the negativity on the outside of the wood-and-mortar structure we are dining in. It blocks out what is happening around the world. For that one evening, we are free from the worries and thankful for family and friends.

Let's face it: there are many, many wonderful men and woman who are great cooks and chefs and who can certainly make delicious meatballs. However, I believe it is Kathy's heart that makes her meatballs so special. She and her husband, Rick, are both kind and always make those in their company feel special. I believe that when Kathy is making a dish, whether it be meatballs or a dessert, her heart and prayers are for all those who will partake of the meal.

In this day and age of uncertainty, increasing hate, and the judgment and rejection of those who are different, Kathy is a beacon who assures those who meet her that love does exist. She radiates compassion to those who need someone to talk to and extends her beautiful smile to those who are sick and to those who need a friend. Just like meatballs and sauce, which take several ingredients to taste delicious, love takes acceptance, compassion, hope, faith, and forgiveness to make a difference in someone's life. Kathy has mastered that, and it shows in the faces of everyone she meets.

Kathy's Meatballs and Gravy (Sauce)

"It all starts with the "gravy." Most people call it spaghetti sauce. I use a can of crushed tomato or tomato puree and a small can of tomato paste.

Put some olive oil in a pot, and warm it a little; add the can of paste and stir it around a few times. Add a can of water. Now add the can of sauce. Add your Italian spices of choice. Preheat oven to four hundred degrees.

Start mixing about two pounds of meat. (Your choice of meat can be a mixture of beef, pork and veal, or plain hamburger. It is up to your preference.) Add two eggs, garlic powder, onion powder, parsley, parmesan cheese, bread crumbs, and pepper. I do not measure the dry ingredients that I add to the meat. Use the amount that your family would like.

Roll the meat into balls and bake until the meatballs are nice and brown. Put the meatballs in the sauce and simmer all day. Serve with your favorite pasta or make meatball sandwiches with good Italian rolls. Add provolone cheese." Enjoy!

Friday: A Day of Lessons

Two years ago, I was asked to help at a funeral luncheon at my church. Of course, I said yes and must admit that it was very rewarding. In fact, it was so rewarding that I continued, always ready to say yes. It was my way of giving back to others who were heartbroken at the loss of a loved one. Sometimes I knew the family, and sometimes I did not. Sometimes the funeral service was held in our church, and sometimes it was not.

Another luncheon to prepare for, another family grieving a loss. Another family I did not know. On this day, the service was held in our church. We worked hard to get everything just right for those joining us for lunch. When we finished with our setup, one of the ladies asked if I wanted to go up to the service. I was unsure if I should since I did not know the family. But my dear friend said it would be okay.

I did not know this beautiful older woman who now resided in heaven. I did not know her family or what she liked or her favorite things to do. I did not know how much she loved her family. As I sat in the pew and watched her casket being pushed down the aisle, the organist played a beautiful hymn, one that I was familiar with. I wondered if it was one of her favorites. As I looked around the church, I did not know how many friends she had and the difference she had made in their lives. I did not know how her influence had helped shape her granddaughter into the young woman she had become. I did not know that she had three daughters who loved her dearly. I did not know that her husband walked with a walker and how much he would miss her loving hands that had helped him for so many years.

After listening to our pastor talk about this sweet woman, I learned what made her so special. I learned about her love for her family, her love of cooking, her beautiful needlework, and how much she loved teaching Sunday school.

Looking around the church, I learned how

many people loved her. I learned just how much her granddaughter loved and admired her grandmother by the loving way she spoke of all the things they had done together. I learned how sad her husband was, grieving for his wife of many years. I learned how much her daughters loved their mother by the tears on their faces.

As I sat and listened to the beautiful message about this special angel, I formed a picture in my mind. I could see her cooking, taking care of her friends, always being there for her family, working with her Sunday-school students, taking care of her husband, and knitting her beautiful blankets. When we sang two of her favorite hymns, I could almost hear her singing along, smiling her warm smile and nodding at a friend. Although I did not know her when I walked into the sanctuary, I left with a new friend in my heart. As I walked down the hall, I celebrated her life with a smile and a feeling of loss for a friend I never had a chance to meet.

The Magic of a Bowl of Soup

This is a story about soup: rich and creamy, chicken and noodles, meat and vegetables, or any recipes you like. Soup warms our bodies and, according to mothers everywhere, heals whatever ails us. Soup can be homemade or made by just opening a can. It can be made in a large pot or in a bowl in the microwave. It is delicious when served with warm crusty bread or crackers. I could go on and on how delicious soup is and how much I like to make it, but there is more to a bowl of soup than just the ingredients, pots, how we cook it, and how we eat it.

Although the above has a lot of merit, there

is so much to know about soup and how it can change the lives of others.

I love people of all ages but am especially fond of seniors, those less fortunate, and children. My husband always tells me that I care about every person I meet. Maybe he is right. I only know that if I can help someone, I will try.

Did you ever realize that some folks who are in need never ask for anything? They struggle in silence. It doesn't matter whether their need is financial or health related. When asked if they need anything, their response is usually, "We're fine," or "I'm fine." My favorite is, "We'll get by." However, the expression on their faces says it all, especially with the elderly. I have two neighbors who come to mind.

I would often ask if they needed a meal or help with errands, but the answer was always the same: "No, thanks. We are okay." I knew in my heart that they were not as I walked away with a feeling of sadness. Then the idea of a bowl of soup started to simmer.

It was a cold, snowy day. A perfect day to make soup. I decided to make twice the amount of my chicken bowtie soup with the hope that my two neighbors would be more inclined to accept it if I told them I had made way too much for my husband and me. I remember calling them up and explaining the predicament I was in and almost pleading for them to take a container to help me out. It worked!

As I delivered each container, I saw their smiles and heard them say, "It smells good! Thank you!" I felt good as I walked home, knowing that they had something hot to eat on a cold winter's night. Soon my phone rang and rounds of "The soup was great! You didn't have to do this, but we are sure glad you did" and "I wish there was a way I could repay you. Maybe someday when things get better" began. Little did they know that they had already repaid me by just being the loving, caring people they were.

I am not telling you this story to brag about my soup-making skill; however, I am sharing in hopes that you, dear reader, will reach out to those in need. Whether it is a neighbor, the homeless, a wounded warrior, or a struggling family member, helping others, it is always the right thing to do.

The Real Magic in a Bowl of Soup…

The real magic of a bowl of soup is simple: it is caring, sharing, and above all love. So, make a pot of soup, and pass the magic on; for when we help others, we truly help ourselves.

Cynthia's Magic Chicken Bowtie Soup

- Four skinned chicken breasts (or any part of the chicken you like)

- Homemade stock or can stock (I use 8 cups or more)
- 6 stalks of celery, diced
- 1 onion, chopped (I use a medium Vidalia onion)
- 6 carrots, diced
- 2 or more potatoes, diced
- Parsley (fresh or dried)
- One box of bowtie noodles (farfalle)
- Salt and pepper to taste

Cook the chicken breasts in the homemade stock or can stock. I usually cover the chicken to start, adding more stock as I add each ingredient. First, add the parsley, celery, and onion. Add more broth. Simmer for a tad, and then add the carrots. Add more broth. When the chicken is cooked, remove from the pot, and let cool. Add the potatoes and cook for about ten minutes. Cut chicken in small pieces and add to the soup mixture. Bring the soup to a boil, and add the noodles (half to one box, depending on how much soup you are making). Stir the noodles, and then turn the temperature down to medium. Cook and stir until the noodles are al dente. Turn off the stove. The heat from the broth will finish cooking the bowtie noodles to perfection. Add more broth if needed. Salt and pepper to taste. Serve with crusty bread. Share with someone you love!

My Dream

One of my favorite movies is *The Sound of Music.* I love the scene when mother superior sings about climbing every mountain until you find your dream.

One of my many dreams is to make a difference with my words. I hope my stories have inspired you to reach out and help others, strive to make a difference, and love and accept all those who cross your path.

Made in the USA
Columbia, SC
01 April 2018